S0-AUY-192

The Ernst & Young Information Management Series

---

60 Minute Software

Also from Ernst & Young

Books for Entrepreneurs:

The Ernst & Young Guide to Taking Your Company Public

The Ernst & Young Guide to Financing for Growth

The Ernst & Young Business Plan Guide, Second Edition

Information Management Series:

Development Effectiveness: Strategies for IS Organizational Transition

Managing Information Strategically: Increase Your Company's Competitiveness and Efficiency by Using Information as a Strategic Tool

Information Technology for Integrated Health Systems: Positioning for the Future

General Reference:

Privatization: Investing in State-Owned Enterprises Around the World

Mergers & Acquisitions, Second Edition

The Ernst & Young Guide to Total Cost Management

The Ernst & Young Guide to Special Event Management

The Name of the Game: The Business of Sports

The Ernst & Young Almanac and Guide to U.S. Business Cities

Holistic Management (forthcoming)

Real-Time Profit Management: Making Your Bottom Line a Sure Thing

Understanding and Using Financial Data: An Ernst & Young Guide for Attorneys

Tax & Personal Finance:

The Ernst & Young Tax Savers' Guide

The Ernst & Young Tax-Saving Strategies Guide

The Ernst & Young Personal Financial Planning Guide

The Ernst & Young Guide to the New Tax Law

The Ernst & Young New York, New Jersey, Connecticut State Tax Guide

The Ernst & Young Information Management Series

60 Minute Software

Strategies for Accelerating the Information Systems Delivery Process

John Parkinson
Ernst & Young LLP

JOHN WILEY & SONS, INC.
New York • Chichester • Brisbane • Toronto • Singapore

This text is printed on acid-free paper.

Published by John Wiley & Sons, Inc.

Library of Congress Cataloging-in-Publication Data:

ISBN 0-471-11503-7

Printed in the United States of America

10 9 8 7 6 5 4 3 2 1

For the second time, this is for Marianne
(for the first time)

Preface

Always remember, none of us alone is as smart as all of us together.

—ROGER NELSON

It's not what you know *you don't know that hurts you, it's what you* don't know *you don't know.*

—JIM MANZI

Everyone knows software takes too long to develop and deliver. Even though the software industry has made giant strides in productivity over the past 25 years, it has consistently failed to keep up with customer demand. This demand has been and continues to be fueled by the technology-led expectation that new software should appear cheaply and more or less "on demand," just as new hardware seems to. Major investments in new tools, processes, and people (either via training or vitality hiring) have made only marginal differences that usually cannot be sustained. The demand for software of all types continues to grow—and is now a common reason cited for the inability of a business to meet new customer, product, or market requirements.

Can anything really be done to improve this situation and, if so, *what*? This book looks at the results of more than three years of observation and research into process accelerators for the Information Systems (IS) development-and-delivery process. It identifies the main problems with cycle time compression and offers strategies to address them. It reviews successes and failures in applying acceleration strategies and points to the lessons to be learned from the efforts of leading IS organizations and the best practices they have developed and deployed.

This research includes input from many sources. The participants in the Acceleration Action Group of E&Y's Information Technology (IT) Leadership multi-client research program; observations from E&Y's own program of accelerated systems development (ASD) projects carried out both internally and for clients; and the results of conversations and correspondence with leading practitioners in the diverse areas covered by rapid development approaches. Some of the conclusions are obvious, some are a surprise, and some could be considered to be controversial. Much conventional wisdom about the IS development process is called into question, none too soon in some cases. What works well in one organization often does not work well elsewhere. What works once is often not repeatable, even by the same team. Buried in the mass of performance data collected from several hundred projects are a few fascinating "truths" about the possibilities for sustained cycle time compression for the IS development-and-delivery process. This book presents these truths in a catalog of acceleration practices that can be tried out in the real world, and a list of deceleration factors to try to avoid.

A word of caution, however. By original *background* I am a mathematician and computer scientist. By *chance* (and circumstance), a methodologist, and by *choice* (and necessity), a pragmatist. I have learned, the hard way, that not everything that works is easy to explain and (worse) not everything that should work actually does. In this book there are many inferences drawn from observations that simply do not have true statistical significance. For one thing, I don't usually get to set-up a rigorous experimental framework to test an improvement hypothesis. For another, we just do not have enough data points to account for the effects of all the known sources of variation in the processes we use. In this sense, many of the conclusions are "unscientific" and this annoys the mathematician in me intensely.

The pragmatist, however, doesn't much care. If it worked once, it's at least worth considering. If it has never worked, don't bother with it (forget that it's a neat idea—life is too short). So treat the contents and conclusions herein with caution—you have been warned.

JOHN PARKINSON

Irving, Texas
November 1995

Acknowledgments

As always, thanks are due to the many people who made this book possible. The participant organizations and their representatives in the Acceleration Action Group of the Ernst & Young LLP (E&Y) IT Leadership program (listed in Appendix 1) all made invaluable contributions to, and observations on, the material on which this book is based. I learned a lot from them. I hope they enjoyed their participation in the program as much as I did. The management group for the IT Leadership Multi-client Research Program, particularly Vaughn Merlyn, Rick Swanborg, Mary Silva Doctor, and Nancy Wendt, colleagues and associates from the E&Y Center for Business Innovation (CBI) in Boston, all made contributions and provided comments and insights as the work progressed. The team and participants in the CBI's other multi-client research programs (Mastering the Information Environment [MIE], Implementing Business Change and Mastering Information and Technology) who were kind enough to invite me to a number of their meetings both broadened and gave depth to this work in ways I had not originally intended. In particular, I would like to thank Tom Davenport (now at the University of Texas at Austin), Larry Prusak, Randy Russell, and Dave DeLong, as well as the MIE program participants from

American Airlines, Hoffman LaRoche, Hughes Space and Communications, American Express Travel Related Services, Hewlett Packard, and Johnson & Johnson.

I must also thank John and Ann Spinetto, at the time the Area Director and Marketing Manager, respectively, for E&Y's Charlotte office Management Consulting practice, who invited me to participate in the Carolinas IS Quality Program that they conceived and developed. The participant companies in this program (listed in Appendix 2) have provided a wide range of insights and supporting data that further fueled my research. I have greatly enjoyed my continuing participation in the program, now in its third year under the able stewardship of Walt McBride.

I was privileged to observe the work of many of my fellow partners and principals in Ernst & Young LLP's U.S. Management Consulting practice (too many to name individually here), as the engagement teams they direct built and delivered critical applications for our clients—often trying out the ideas presented in this book in the real world for the first time. Their understanding and trust made much of this research possible. Their (and their clients') willingness to innovate the applications software development-and-delivery process and their forbearance when my research and development team did not get everything quite right is one of the great continuing strengths of our business.

I must also thank my colleagues and the members of my research and development teams at the E&Y Center for Business Transformation in Las Colinas, Texas: Rich Barie, Roy Youngman (now with Boston Chicken Inc.), Carrie Phillips, Stacy Barie, John Lusk, Steve Biroshik, John Bartlett, and Bonnie Schneir. All worked extraordinarily hard as members of the acceleration practices research and support teams—despite having continual, conflicting demands (mostly from me) for their time and talents. Steve Ingram, and the members of the Methods Fusion team that he and Greg Stratis co-directed, provided reviews and comments on our work, despite their own busy schedules. Bob Phillips and his team of process-improvement coaches (particularly Tony Clarke, Scott Shultz, Dan Butler, Steve Dages, and Jerry Blocher) provided me with many of the examples that illustrate the problems and solutions discussed throughout the book. This work is the better for all of their insights and input. Any errors in interpretation of their thoughts and ideas are mine.

Finally, thanks are due to Alan Stanford, formerly National Director of Information Technology for E&Y's National Management Consulting Office, David Shpilberg, who succeeded Alan, and the other members of Ernst & Young's U.S. Management Consulting Management Committee for sponsoring and supporting the original internal and multi-client research work, and for their permission and encouragement to write this book.

J.P.

Contents

Part III Acceleration Strategies for Information Systems Delivery

Part IV Conclusions: How Fast Can We Really Get?

PART I

The Quest for Cycle Time Compression in Software Development

1

Introduction

In their book *Competing against Time*[1] George Stalk, Jr. and Thomas Hout, of the Boston Consulting Group, made a compelling case for the competitive advantage that accrues to the first organization to market with a new idea, product, or service. Many organizations have taken on this "strategy of speed," creating the capability to do things quickly as a fundamental part of their search for sustainable success in increasingly complex and rapidly changing markets.

In an earlier book, *Competing in Time*,[2] Peter Keen, the executive director of the International Center for Information Technologies in Washington, D.C., made an equally strong case for the role of telecommunications technologies—essentially high-speed information handling—in creating and sustaining competitive advantage. Keen's thesis, although it predates the publication by Stalk and Hout, extends their vision of speed to market with the associated perspective that being the *first to know* that something can or must be done is as important as being the *first to do it*.

In an excellent analysis of technology-leveraged process reengineering, *Process Innovation: Reengineering Work through Information Technology*,[3] Tom Davenport describes a variety of ways in which Information Technology can radically improve the effectiveness and efficiency of business processes. Using technology-enabled process redesign, Davenport cites many examples of radical improvement in process operation and the accompanying challenges in organizational and cultural transition.

In *The Corporation of the 1990s*,[4] edited by Michael Scott Morton, a vision of the organizational transformations available to companies that master Information Technology is convincingly developed by the book's eight groups of contributors.

[1] *Competing against Time*, by George Stalk, Jr. and Thomas M. Hout. New York: Free Press, 1990.

[2] *Competing in Time*, by Peter G.W. Keen. New York: Harper Business Books, 1988.

[3] *Process Innovation: Reengineering Work through Information Technology*, by Thomas H. Davenport. Boston: Harvard Business School Press, 1992.

[4] *The Corporation of the 1990s: Information Technology and Organizational Transformation*, ed. by Michael S. Scott Morton. New York: Oxford University Press, 1991.

In *Fast Cycle Time: How to Align Purpose, Strategy, and Structure for Speed,*[5] Christopher Meyer, Managing Director of the Strategic Alignment Group, presents a case study in the creation of an effective, short cycle time enterprise and points out how such an organization is able to compete in rapidly changing markets. Meyer's thesis: "Be fast or be last."

As businesses redesign their core processes to be fast, flexible in operation, and responsive to the demands of their customers, information technology and the information-handling and management systems that it make possible have come to play a central role in achieving significant and sustained cycle time compression. This applies, at least where the Information Systems (IS) organization has been able to build and deliver the required systems fast enough.

The long history of most IS organizations' failure to deliver critical information systems on time and on budget has been well-chronicled elsewhere and will not be repeated here.[6] It is sufficient to note, however, that the timely delivery and implementation of new or significantly improved information systems is now a major bottleneck for organizations seeking to re-engineer their core processes to meet the needs of the "new global marketplace." Before exploring how to fix this critical issue, we'll start with some important background.

Lessons from Lean Manufacturing

The economies-of-scale in mass production, invented in the early 20th century and first implemented on a large scale in the automo-

[5] *Fast Cycle Time: How to Align Purpose, Strategy, and Structure for Speed,* by Christopher Meyer. New York: Free Press, 1993.

[6] See, for instance, *Development Effectiveness: Strategies for IS Organizational Transition,* by Vaughn Merlyn and John Parkinson. New York: John Wiley & Sons, 1994.

bile industry, fundamentally changed the relationship between person and process in manufacturing. Volume of demand for products quickly saturated the traditional manufacturing capabilities of individuals or small groups, and forced a fundamental redesign of the manufacturing process. The resulting processes treated people as if they were machines. The economic design of these processes assumed that labor was the biggest contributor to cost and therefore required that the efficiency of labor be maximized. Although early gains over "craft" processes were significant, they proved not to be sustainable once factors such as product quality and customer preferences became critical.

Failures of the Mass-Production Model for Manufacturing

Mass production certainly achieves economies-of-scale, but human beings, especially in Western cultures that espouse individualist philosophies and values, do not respond well to the requirements for the sustained operation of overly mechanistic processes. As a result, quality is difficult to maintain unless the process can be completely automated. Where complete automation is not possible, the bureaucracies that grow up to address quality failures add further inefficiencies. Eventually, classical mass-production methods fail to remain competitive with more innovative participative manufacturing processes, even when unit costs comparisons seem to favor the mass-production methods.

Total Quality Issues and the Relationship between Defects and Morale

Early pioneers in the quality movement recognized that many of the ills of mass-production systems were *process* failures.[7] Although

[7]See, for example, the extensive work of Juran, Demming, and Crosby.

much of their remedial work centered on process controls, they also pointed out the need to re-engage production workers with the quality-related needs of the production process. Getting the producers involved—so that quality of work mattered to everyone—was as important to successful mass production as statistical process control, defect-prevention schemes, and improved process automation. Production workers could only deliver sustained levels of product quality and process productivity *if they wanted to.*

Mass Production vs. the Work Cell Model

Production management began to address the quality problems of mass-production lines by re-engaging production workers with their work processes—by making them *process owners.* From these initiatives have come the flexible manufacturing and team-oriented production processes that leading manufacturers use today.[8] In these processes it is common for a single team of production workers to complete each product (even complex, high-engineering-content products) from raw materials or components, to finished and tested form. Team members have specific job skills and associated roles, combined with varying degrees of cross-training that provide for flexibility in work processes. In many instances these new approaches have dramatically reversed the decline in product quality and made previously high-cost manufacturing processes competitive with the much lower unit cost traditional processes used by competitors.

Given these successes, there is a strong tempation to take the same "work-cell" approach with software developers. Create small teams of developers within which each team member would have a specific skill and role, with appropriate cross-training. In adopting

[8] For an absorbing description of the MIT five-year study into the reinvention of the automobile industry by the Japanese automakers, see *The Machine That Changed the World: The Story of Lean Production*, by James P. Womack, Daniel T. Jones, and Daniel Roos. New York: Harper Perennial, 1991.

this approach we would try to solve the software quality and productivity dilemma by moving straight to these "software development cells," and thus avoid the problems experienced in the 1970s and 1980s with the first generations of production-line–like software factories.[9] Indeed, strong arguments have been put forward in support of this approach.[10,11]

Why Software Is Not Like Automobiles

Developing this work-cell approach to software manufacture is a seductive and seemingly credible idea. By adopting processes that have already proven successful in analogous "production" situations, it is possible to avoid the uncertainties of radical process re-engineering and gain useful leverage in getting started. The problem, however, is that building software, particularly sophisticated business-support software, is not yet like building cars or even CD players. It is arguable that it never will be. (Actually, I don't believe this myself, but I have no proof that the skeptics are wrong, and there are compelling theoretical and empirical arguments to support their viewpoint.)

Causal Models of the Production Process and Sources of Variability

With cars (and most other manufactured products) there exists a "model" of the manufacturing process that is "complete" in many important ways. It allows the design of a production process that is deterministic—it can be known completely what has to be done before starting. There is an optimum order for manufacture and

[9] See *Japan's Software Factories*, by Michael A. Cusumano. New York: Oxford University Press, 1991.

[10] *The Software Factory: Managing Software Development and Maintenance*, by James R. Robinson. Wellesley, MA: QED Information Sciences Inc., 1991.

[11] *The Database Factory*, by Stephen G. Schur. New York: John Wiley & Sons, 1994.

assembly (which can be determined in advance, perhaps by experimentation), and sources of possible variation. Manufacturing tolerances and assembly errors, for instance, can be detected and controlled using statistical sampling methods or exhaustive examination.

Predictability of Outcome

We therefore have an ability to predict the outcome of the process, to measure the quality of what is produced, and to design feedback loops that ensure that the process remains within "control," despite sources of variability during execution.

In classical design engineering and product manufacturing systems, we can, at least in theory, discover everything we need to know about the product to be made before making it. With modern computer-aided design (CAD) and manufacturing technology, all of the design engineering required can be done without actually building anything "real" at all. This capability can be applied even to very large and complex production processes. In contrast to traditional airframe design processes, Boeing's Commercial Aircraft Group created the complete design for the new Boeing 777 twin-jet passenger aircraft entirely on a CAD system. No scale models were built. The first plane to be built in the test series was actually the first to fly. Similarly, Boston's Central Artery Project, redirecting the major through-routes for road traffic into tunnels beneath the city, was extensively modeled on a computer system prior to actual construction planning.

Once the design is complete, a "bill of materials" can be constructed for the product, as well as a plan for material requirements, and a procedure for component assembly—even for extremely complex "systems" with millions of components and demanding safety and performance characteristics. The work can be scheduled so that production processes are optimized in any of several ways (time, cost, resource consumption, and so on). Using this approach, efficient and flexible manufacturing processes can be designed.

Patterns of Discovery

Software development is seldom like this. We can't usually "discover" everything we need to know in the exact order we need to know it. Awareness of what is possible evolves through participation in the requirements discovery process and, consequently, requirements change and designs must be changed to remain consistent with better articulated needs. Decisions, however rational or "correct" they may have been when made, have to be reversed. Schedules must be changed in unpredictable ways, and other variables must be identified and managed as they occur.

Many of the process characteristics that allow manufacturing systems to work flexibly and effectively are often absent from software development.[12] Building software is much more like the processes used by specialist job shops. Here, relatively few copies of a product are ever made; every execution of the manufacturing process is a little different, even for the same product; the work almost always requires skilled and experienced craftspeople; there is much trial and error; little reusability results; and the process costs are high.

Lessons from Mass Customization

Software development is not, however, the only "manufacturing" process that has these unfavorable characteristics. The lessons of uncertainty and discovery are being learned again in the shift toward mass-customization strategies and the "batch size of one" approaches to product manufacturing.[13] As we try to make as many characteristics of our products as individually customizable as possi-

[12] See *Exploiting Chaos*, by Dave Olsen. VNR Computer Library. New York: Van Nostrand Reinhold, 1993.

[13] "Making Mass Customization Work," by B.J. Pine, B. Victor, and A.C. Boynton. *Harvard Business Review*, September, 1993.

ble, we are once again being forced to sacrifice production efficiency (and productivity) to maintain quality. Hence the unit cost and cycle time gains from the last decade are being eroded.

It is against this background of experience, both good and bad, that the search begins for ways to improve the fundamental speed of the software delivery process. There are important lessons to be learned from all three generations of mass-production experience—both in what we should consider doing and what we should avoid.

Lessons from Re-engineering

Over the past five years or so, many companies have employed the practice and process of re-engineering for the radical redesign of their business processes. The re-engineering experience has generated an extensive literature and much anecdotal material.[14–16] Although there were many early failures, more recent results suggest that much can and is being accomplished using re-engineering approaches. Re-engineering uses technology (often information technology) and human-resource–related levers to transform the way people operate a process, often producing significant improvements in cycle time and cost. There are, however, important consequences for those who must implement the new processes and the technologies that support them.

As redesigned business processes get more streamlined, their operation (and inter-operation) tends to get more complex and must be much more tightly integrated with the information flows that they use and the technologies that are developed to support these flows. Successful implementation is increasingly dependent on hav-

[14] *Innovation and Entrepreneurship*, by Peter F. Drucker. New York: Harper & Row, 1985.

[15] *Reengineering the Corporation. A Manifesto for Business Revolution*, by Michael Hammer and James Champy. New York: Harper Business, 1993.

[16] *Innovation: The Attacker's Advantage*, by Foster Richard. London: Macmillan, 1986.

ing all of the necessary components available exactly when they are needed. This tends to increase the critical mass of components for which just-in-time delivery must be synchronized.

Having components show up late is an obvious inconvenience that can add considerable cost when the scope of deployment is large, even if the delay is small. What's not so obvious is that having things show up *before* they are needed is also a problem. Inventory-management facilities must be provided for the delivered components until they are needed, or until it is possible to use them. This is especially true when a developed information system arrives before the customer is ready to implement it. The ideal is true "just-in-time" availability for the informational (and information-technology–based) components of the re-engineered processes.

2

Issues with Cycle Time Compression

Remember, gravity isn't just a good idea—it's the law.
—DAVID HANNIGAN

In the wake of the business re-engineering wave of the early 1990s, it has seemingly become conventional wisdom that the cycle time for any process can be first radically and then continuously improved. In most peoples' thinking, and in much of the cycle time compression literature, this improvement is presented as though it can go on forever. In practice this is seldom, if ever, true. In some cases, the characteristics of the process severely limit the degree to which cycle times can be compressed safely and successfully.

Cycle Times That Can't Be Compressed

A good example of a process that can't really be compressed successfully is the playing of music. When Mozart first wrote *Piano Concerto No. 19*, he had only poorly fed and trained musicians to play it and they generally had poorly manufactured instruments. In those days it took about 26½ minutes to play the piece. Now, many years later, there are much better instruments and much healthier and better trained musicians. How long does the Mozart concerto now take to play? Still 26½ minutes.

Of course, we can always speed up the music. The players can play faster, although there are obviously physical limits to this particular "speed-up" approach. We can also apply technology—record the musicians playing at normal speed and then speed-up the playback as much as desired (there are, of course, limits here, too, although these are *less* limiting than those that once bound human performance and are—Doppler effects for example—much less obvious). The only trouble with this approach is that the result no longer sounds like the music we started with—and no one wants to listen to it (nor could we, in the most extreme case, actually hear it).

What can be learned from this? The lesson here is that some processes have characteristics in time that are, necessarily, *invariant*. To change these characteristics is to have a different process or a different outcome—or both.

What was lost by the compression? Despite the fact that all the data in the original score were preserved (there are no "lost" notes and the order of playing did not change), other characteristics (such as the rhythm—as determined by the gaps between the notes and the duration of each note) were altered, and the result was the loss of the original intent and of the musical experience. We need to be sure that processes we attempt to compress don't have characteristics that behave in a similar fashion, thwarting our attempts to reduce their cycle time.

Cycle Times That Shouldn't Be Compressed

Let's use eating a meal as an example. There is really no need to separate out the various "courses" of a meal. The fact that we do so is a combination of convenience, custom, and aeshetics. We could just pile all of the "components" of a meal in a heap on the plate and go at it (children and some adults seem to do this, anyway). This potentially speeds-up the eating process, but most would agree that it also detracts from the quality of the dining experience.

Such an approach can also cause related processes—in this case, digestion—that have their own implicit cycle times, to go awry. If food was just fuel, we would probably not bother with the elaborate and time-consuming eating rituals we use. If digestion was not a complex, time- and capacity-controlled chemical transformation process, eating could be greatly simplified. But digestion is a relatively slow process and the capacity of our digestive tract is limited. It therefore makes sense to synchronize the rate of intake (eating) to the effective capacity and rate of the digestive process. As a result we have come to regard food as more than just fuel—as a component in a wider and more complex social process that has its own pace and expectations of experience. So we separate out sets of flavors and take longer than we need to eat.

What can be learned from this? The full "value" of eating as a process is not just represented by the nutritional value of the food we eat. The capacity and rate characteristics for related processes must be examined to actually assess the value of the eating process. To retain this value we must accept that the process will take time—and plan accordingly.

What was lost by the attempt at cycle time compression? Lost are not only the aesthetics of the eating experience, but there are practical possibilities for loss as well. If the human digestive system's capacity is exceeded, we become ill to varying degrees and can lose some or all of the nutritional value from the food eaten.

That doesn't mean that some aspects of the eating process's cycle time can't be compressed if they are not important to us. The preparation and delivery parts of the process are a good example. "Fast" food is a much larger industry in the United States than is restaurant dining (which, notice, we don't generally call "slow" food, although it often qualifies for such a label), with dramatically reduced cycle times for preparation and delivery, as well as lower process costs. Is it the same eating experience? Not exactly, but it does generally serve the same process need.

What to Do when Something Can't Be Compressed but Must Be

There is a group exercise (called "group juggle") that we use to help show a group of people that they often don't recognize how to speed-up a process. They make limiting assumptions about the process that are reasonable, but unnecessary. Once these assumptions have been challenged (generally using a participative experimentation or discovery learning process) the improvements that can be achieved are "amazing" and easy to get. In this exercise, the group discovers how to reduce a complex and error-prone process, that takes usually about 120 seconds, to a simple, error-free process that can be completed in less than one tenth of a second—an improvement of three orders of magnitude in less than ten minutes elapsed time.

Neither trick nor "sleight of hand" is involved. The group does it by inventing a new process with the same objectives as the old one, but with all irrelevant constraints removed. We call this "thinking outside the nine dots" (see Figure 2.1), or "getting outside of the box."

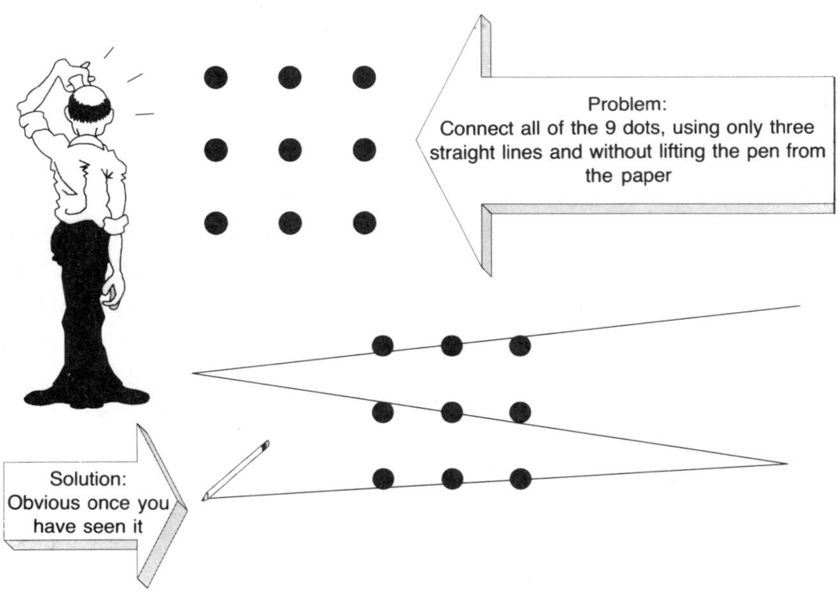

Figure 2.1 *The "nine dots" puzzle and its "outside-the-dots" solution.*

What can be learned from this? Sometimes there is no choice but to innovate. More often than not, if you have to innovate, you discover that you can. As we shall see, innovation also gets easier with practice.[1]

There remain, however, the problems of "in-flight" process change. As a final piece of the exercise, we have the group change from the old, slow process to the new rapid one, *while still operating the old process.* Chaos immediately ensues. In-flight process change is much harder to do than is the design of the new process itself. This is the first of several lessons that will demonstrate that implementation, not innovation, remains the real challenge.

Why Faster Is Not Always Better

Transformation Functions and Rate Limits

Let's return for a moment to the food metaphor used earlier and look at processes for cooking. Cooking is a good example of a time-constrained transformation process. It takes about 12 minutes at 325°F to cook a medium-rare steak. It's reasonable to assume that the total energy input to the process is a key determinant of the outcome. Suppose we decide to double the temperature and halve the time, which essentially maintains the total energy input.[2] Would you want to eat the result?

What can be learned from this? Sometimes the laws of nature dictate the rate at which important transformations occur. Protein hydrolization and fat carbonization occur at optimum rates that

[1]For a discussion on the processes involved in breaking people away from old concepts and creating a new awareness of what is possible, see *Future Edge: Discovering the New Paradigms of Success*, by Joel A. Barker. New York: William Morrow and Company, 1992.

[2]This is an approximation. The actual relationship between temperature and radiated energy is not linear.

require specific physical conditions to trigger the transformational process. Without these conditions, either nothing happens (you can't cook a steak at 100°F, no matter how long you try) or there is a dramatically different result. At 1000°F the outside of the steak quickly chars to almost pure carbon, but the inside remains raw.[3] At 10,000°F the steak is rapidly converted to oxides of carbon and nitrogen, water vapor, and trace organic gases; at 100,000°F the steak becomes a dissociated plasma, and so on. If the band of physical parameters within which the desired transformation is possible gets ignored the transformation process just won't work as expected, or won't work at all.

What was lost when things were speeded up? In this case, the required end-state of the process—an edible steak. Notice, however, that the laws of physics give a number of ways to supply the energy needed to cook the steak and, by choosing the appropriate form of conduction, convection, or irradiation, the time over which the application occurs can be varied. Instead of applying energy as radiated or convected heat, other forms can be used to get a faster result. By using radio frequency energy instead of infrared, we can "heat" the steak by "shaking" all the water molecules so that they all move a little faster and the meat becomes hotter. This is how microwave ovens work.

Once again, however, we had to innovate and change both the process and the technology used. And, even so, we didn't get quite the same deliverable. The steak cooked and will taste just fine, but it doesn't *look* quite the same.

Threshold Conditions and Quantum Changes

There is another class of changes to be aware of when looking at cycle time compression strategies. Some processes have characteristics that cause them first to be insensitive to changes over a wide range of control values, but then to change suddenly once a

[3] Because carbon is such a good insulator.

threshold value is reached. When we encounter such a process, we need to know where we are in relation to the threshold, because the amount of effort we put into cycle time compression may:

- Have no result, if we are far from the threshold value; or
- Be wasteful (more than needed) if we are to close the threshold.

We will want to apply just the amount of effort required to move from the initial state of the process to the threshold in order to minimize wasted effort. Figure 2.2 shows examples of this

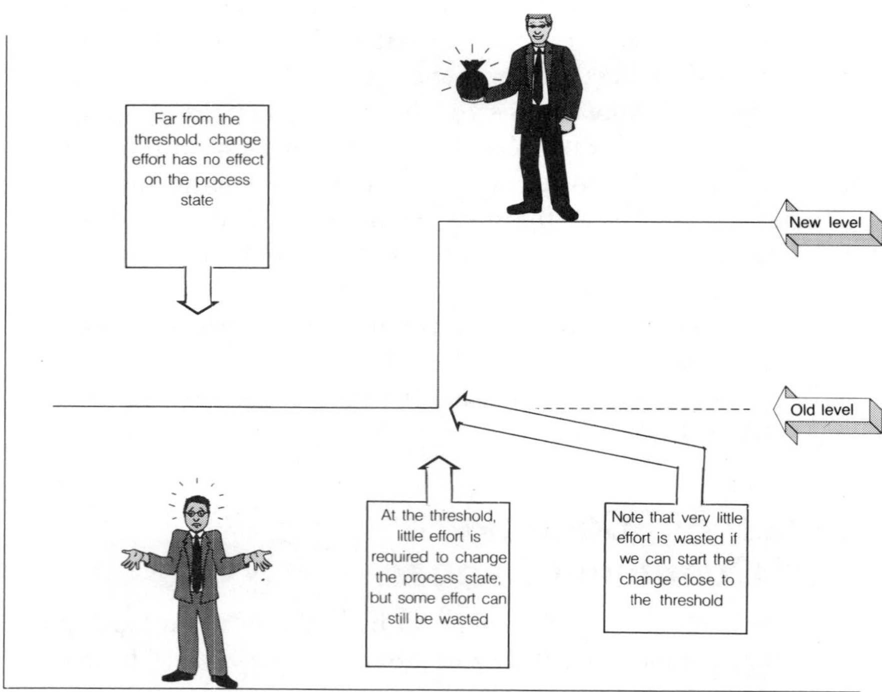

***Figure 2.2** Proximity to the threshold determines the effect of a specific change effort.*

principle. An important corollary of this situation occurs when we get the change effects we want, so long as we do not exceed the threshold value. But we destroy the process if the value is exceeded.

There are many real-world examples of this phenomenon, particularly where cycle times are squeezed as close as possible to a minimum, and then forced past a critical value without any accompanying process innovation. At that point, the process breaks. This is analogous to the elastic behavior of strong materials. Up to a point, the material compresses (or stretches) as expected in a predictable way. Then, as the elastic limit is reached, the material undergoes a phase change and fails spectacularly and suddenly. Figure 2.3 illustrates this principle.

Indivisibility of Effect Issues

We are all familiar with the old joke that tells us that it is impossible to speed-up human gestation by dividing up the usual nine months of pregnancy among nine women, who take only one month each. Similarly, if we return to the musical analogy, a piece of music can't be played faster by using additional musicians or, for example, playing the first and second halves of the score simultaneously.

There are many other processes that exhibit this characteristic of indivisibility. We have to recognize that, if the work cannot be divided up among multiple resources and carried out in parallel, we will never be able to use many of the most commonly available cycle time reduction strategies.

Even if the work can be divided up, we will need to ensure that this coordination effort does not overwhelm the gains achieved from the division of effort.

Chaos Theory, Uncertainty, and Other Laws of Nature

Finally, we must be on the lookout for processes that, as we reduce their cycle times, have unexpected side-effects in unexpected places.

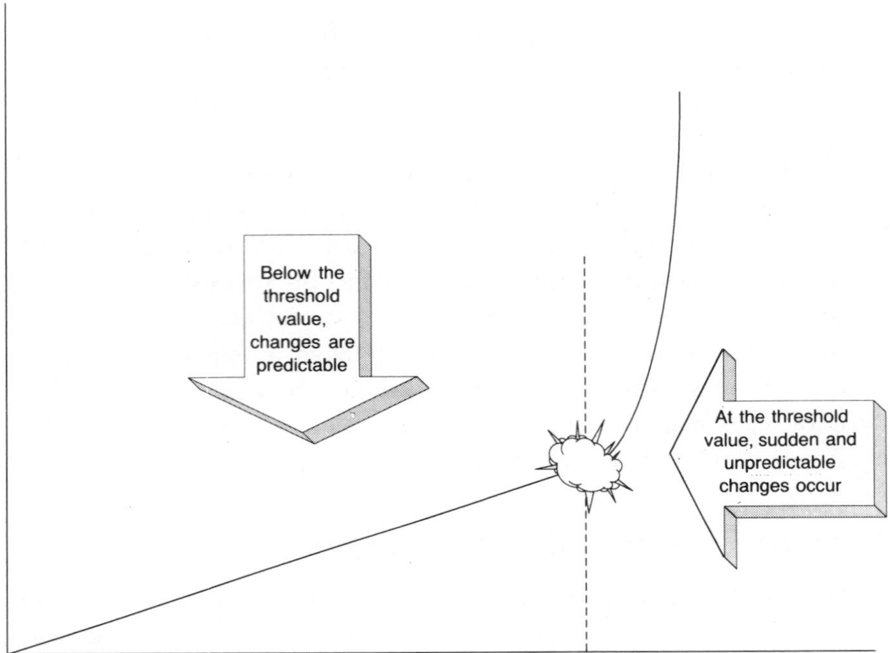

Figure 2.3 *Behavior past the threshold can be unexpectedly different.*

You will probably be familiar with the popular example of a *chaotic effect*, where a single flap of a butterfly's wing in Africa eventually causes a hurricane in the Pacific Ocean. What this story tries to illustrate is the presence of a complex, dynamic set of causal interconnections that exists in most large-scale systems. Not all of these interconnections can be understood or predicted in advance because they change in unpredictable ways and may not even *exist* in advance. If we cannot fully understand the linkages between components in a system, we cannot predict all of the impacts that a change to one component may have on other components, in other parts of the system, at other times.

By speeding-up some parts of a process, we may actually slow other parts down, or cause malfunctions in unexpected places. In his book *The Fifth Discipline*, Peter Senge uses an example in which seemingly rational decisions made in one part of a process propagate changes at different rates to other parts of the same and related processes, eventually causing an apparent failure of the set of processes as a whole.[4] In Senge's example, decisions based on a local viewpoint that failed to consider the consequences of a change on the whole process (or "system") was to blame and Senge argues, quite correctly, that a "systems thinking" approach can help to avoid these errors.

Unfortunately, there are practical limits to the applicability of systems thinking approaches when applied to very large-scale, rapidly executing, complex processes.[5] Although speeding-up parts of a process (especially the informational parts) often reduces timing-lag induced errors of the sort that Senge describes, it can also induce new forms of synchronization error and exaggerate feedback effects that would otherwise dampen out in a slower version of the process.

Chaos theory also describes a type of process within which we can identify the threshold at which a change occurs, but not which state, of several possible resulting states, will result from the change. Alternatively we may encounter a process where we can determine the resulting state, but not which of several possible threshold values will trigger the change. Such process changes have uncertain outcomes or threshold values that are determined by random or seemingly unconnected aspects of the time or place in which the change actually occurs.

Finally we need to remember that all processes are, to some extent, subject to limits that are determined not by what we would like to be possible, but by the laws of nature. If we run into one of these limits, no amount of *process* innovation can help. Instead we will need to find a fundamentally different way to achieve the

[4] *The Fifth Discipline: The Art and Practice of the Learning Organization*, by Peter M. Senge. New York: Doubleday/Currency, 1990, pp. 27–40.

[5] *The Dreams of Reason: The Computer and the Rise of the Sciences of Complexity*, by Heinz R. Pagels. New York: Bantam Books, 1989.

result we want—essentially *concept* innovation, which is a much more difficult requirement even than process innovation. This situation is often extremely inconvenient and, as a result, we will usually be reluctant to acknowledge it. However, if we don't notice that it happened, we can waste a lot of time and effort for no possible gain.

3

The Problem with History

The problem with the future is that it's not what it used to be.
—Yogi Berra

Those that cannot remember the past are condemned to repeat it.
—George Santayana

Every time history repeats itself, the price goes up.
—Anonymous

One of the key lessons from the "paradigm shifting" exercises such as the group juggle described in the previous section is that past experience is not necessarily the best guide to the design of the future state process. If we are too rooted in the "current state" it is very difficult to conceive of a radically different "future state" that does not suffer from current and past limitations on what it can do. The processes and techniques that allow people to break free of the past (usually called "visioning" or something similar) work best when the participants are provided with a few simple tools to help them understand what the components of an effective future state vision need to be. Here are some of the tools and ideas that may be used to help break people free of the past.

Who Do You Want to Be?

In a 1993 article in the *Harvard Business Review*,[1] Michael Treacy introduced the idea of "customer intimacy" and contrasted it with two other strategies for developing effective long-term customer satisfaction, creating customer loyalty and thus gaining "annuity" customers. Treacy characterizes the three strategies as follows.

[1]Customer Intimacy and Other Value Disciplines, by M.E. Treacy and F.D. Wiersma. *Harvard Business Review*, January/February 1993.

Operational Effectiveness—Being the Low-Cost Producer

Businesses that choose this approach tend to have efficient processes producing commodity products where price or availability or a combination of the two are primary buying determinants. As a result, they are seldom innovative cultures and, because they aim to serve many customers, do not invest in specific-customer relationships.

Product Innovation—The Source of the Best New Ideas

Product innovators must constantly push at the bounds of what is possible—work at or beyond the leading edge of practice, and must generate many possible ideas for each one that works. All their energy goes into creation, with little left over for production efficiency or relationship management.

Customer Intimacy— The Trusted Advisor

Businesses that focus on customer intimacy invest in creating and maintaining close relationships with their customers. They are always around to help or are at least accessible whenever their advice is needed. To be available on demand implies that they cannot be committed to work elsewhere. As a result, their processes cannot be operationally excellent from an efficiency perspective and they must temper their degree of innovation to match the constraints of their customers' cultures and needs.

This "triad" of ideas, which we call "the Identity Triad," can be presented graphically, as shown in Figure 3.1. Treacy proposes that all enterprises can be rated somewhere on a scale from "poor" through "good" to "the best" on each of these three axes. The successful enterprise will select one axis to focus on being the best,

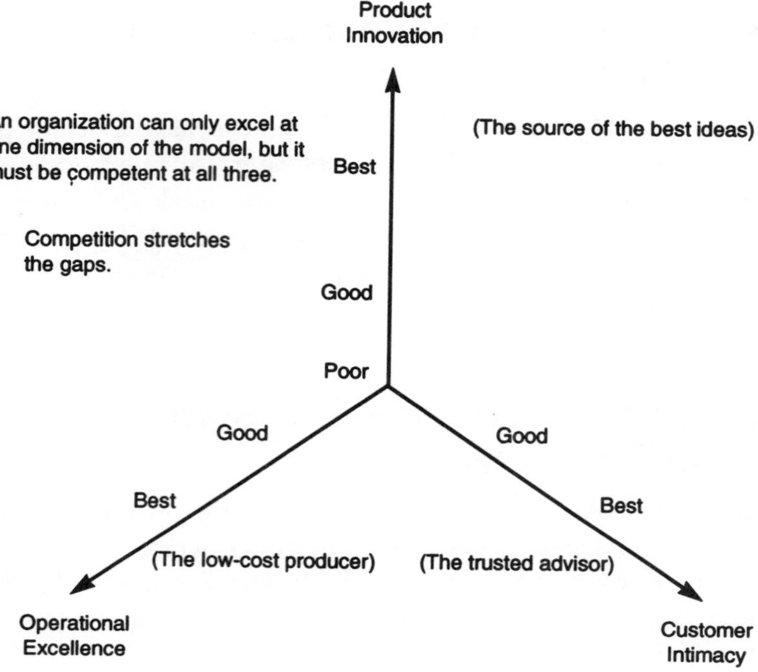

Figure 3.1 *Strategic approaches for continuing customer retention.*

and will try to ensure that it is at least as good as the average of all its competitors (or, perhaps, the average of everyone who is at least "good" in any industry or market) as the other two. Treacy also notes that the definitions of "good" and "the best" change over time as the leaders in each area strive to stay ahead of each other, so no one can rest on current or past success. Finally, Treacy points out that the operational and cultural differences implied by the model make it effectively impossible for any enterprise to be "the best" on all three axes simultaneously—hence the need to select an axis of primary focus. So, if you can't be good at everything (and, according to Treacy's research conclusions, you can't), on which axis will you choose to focus? This is the first issue in defining the shape of the future state and it is as relevant for the Information Systems (IS) organization as for the enterprise as a whole.

The Challenge of Customer Diversity

Matching who you want to be with what your customers want you to be may present a significant challenge. First of all, you have to know what it is your customers *actually do want* from you. During our research we came across a number of situations where the ambitions of the IS organization were completely misaligned with the desires of the parent company that it served. Most commonly, the IS organization wanted to be world-class product innovators, while the parent company wanted a "no-hassles" low-cost producer. In one or two cases, the IS organization had nearly achieved its excellence objectives, but could not understand why its customers were still dissatisfied.

Even if the IS organization understands the need to align with its customers' perceptions of what it should be, there may be difficult issues to reconcile. Multiple conflicting customer expectations are common. Few organizations have so cohesive an internal organization and culture that all internal customer groups have the same perception of what their IS organization should be. In the few examples of an effective, uniform corporate culture that we saw (WalMart is perhaps the best known, large-scale example), the IS organization was able to achieve a great deal simply because it could focus on excellence in the clearly articulated and most appropriate dimension of the triad.

The Moving Target Problem

Even if the IS organization does get a clear and singular direction in which to excel and achieves the excellence objective, it can't rest on past successes. Competitors who made the same choice will constantly try to improve their own performance and, in doing so, will continuously tend to extend the definition of "best" in any dimension. As each axis stretches, the definition of "good," which is the target on any nonstrategic dimension, also gets more difficult to achieve.

As an example, we tracked the measures of "good" and "excellent" for the product innovation axis (the easiest to get consistent data over an extended period) for a number of IS organizations in our study group that identified this axis as their focus. We used as measures:

- The time it took to get a new idea, process, or technology from initial identification to widespread (but not necessarily universal) deployment among the target population; and
- The number of new ideas, processes, and technologies that were considered in any given 12-month period, even if they were not adopted.

These measures tested both the capacity of the organization to create collateral in its focus area and its ability to make good picks among the available collateral. We discovered that, to remain a leader for a decade (from 1982 to 1992), an organization would have had to decrease the time it took to introduce and deploy new collateral by two thirds, and would have had to increase its capacity to generate and evaluate new collateral by more than 12 times. On the product innovation axis, the scores achieved by the leaders in 1982 would not even have qualified as "good" ten years later.

A successful IS organization must therefore continuously improve its performance in all areas if it is to remain among the leaders.

Stratification Consequences

The situation becomes even more complex and challenging if a single axis of focus can't be selected, because different groups of customers want different things. It's possible to set up different groups within the IS organization that each focus on a different dimension of the triad, but it vastly complicates the organizational structure and makes it essentially impossible to manage everyone the same way. The specific processes and behaviors that make for excellence in operational efficiency directly conflict with those needed for excellence in customer intimacy, and so on. Moving staff and managers between groups with a different focus becomes difficult, or impossible, adversely affecting the economies of scope and scale available to the IS organization. Applying uniform performance measures to the different groups is also close to impossible.

So, although a stratification approach is theoretically possible, we did not find anyone who had really been able to make it work for a sustained period of time.

Strategic Alignment

A successfully functioning organization must constantly balance the effectiveness of the processes it uses, the technology that supports them, and the skills and competencies of the people that must work with these processes and technologies. Maintaining this balance requires constant adjustment. Figure 3.2 illustrates the critical issues.

If an organization focuses too much on any one of the three dimensions of the model, for example, innovating processes without updating technology and retraining staff, the model will rapidly become unbalanced. The "pressure" applied to the process area will tend to force the other two areas (technology and people) apart, and the potential benefits from an innovated process will be reduced, or lost.

Similar effects occur if new technology is introduced without corresponding changes to the processes that it supports and the skills and working practices of the people who must use it.

To achieve alignment, we must seek to apply pressure to all

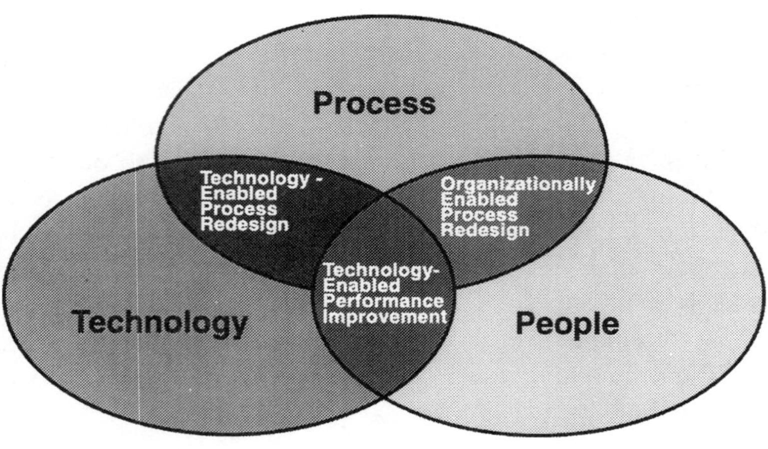

Figure 3.2 *The strategic alignment model.*

three areas at once or, at worst, to move rapidly from one area to the next, applying enough pressure to keep all three areas in balance. We call this the "balance of forces" model of strategic alignment, and it is a challenging management requirement because of the dynamic nature and constantly changing focus of the management processes that it implies.

Creating strategic alignment implies maximizing the synergistic effects that occur when people, processes, and technology work well together. Ideally, we would like to apply simultaneous improvements and innovations to all three areas, but this is seldom possible. Instead, we must usually settle for a consistent cycle of change, with improvement attention moving rapidly from, for example, process to technology to people. Whatever sequence we use, value creation occurs when we can create and maintain the maximum synergy between the people, process, and technology areas.

Mapping the Strategic Alignment Model to the Identity Triad

We can combine the concepts represented by the Treacy model of strategic identity with the ideas of strategic alignment to select the best combination of approach and identity. Figure 3.3 illustrates this combination.

If we choose *Operational Excellence* as our strategic identity, we will need to focus initially on the *process* dimension and plan to support improved processes with appropriate technology and working practices, incentives, and organizational behaviors.

If we choose *Product Innovation*, we will need a technology

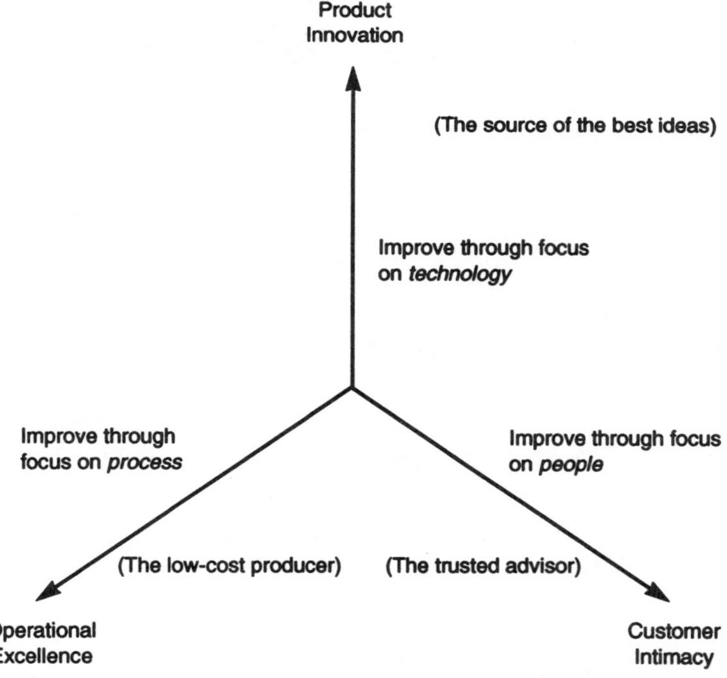

Figure 3.3 *Mapping the identity triad to the strategic alignment model.*

dimension focus with appropriate competencies and cultural reinforcement, supported by technology-enabled and -efficient processes.

Finally, if our objective is *Customer Intimacy*, we will need an initial people dimension focus, supported by appropriate processes and technology.

This combination of strategic identity and strategic alignment allows us both to decide who we want to be and to get started on creating business process, an organizational structure, and a technology environment that will support our objectives.

Distinguishing between Efficiency and Effectiveness

In many of the organizations that we observed (more than 85% of the companies in our study group), improvement efforts were focused almost exclusively on improving the *productivity* of the IS organization. We characterized these improvements as "efficiency focused"—aimed at "doing things right"—usually with the idea of doing things right the first time.

In a smaller group (about 10% of participants), the focus was almost exclusively on learning more about what the IS organization's customers actually wanted. We characterized these efforts as "effectiveness focused"—aimed at "doing the right things."

Only in about 5 percent of participants was there a conscious articulation that both types of improvements were required and had to be addressed simultaneously.

Doing Things Right vs. Doing the Right Things

This distinction may not, at first, seem important, but a focus on just a single direction of improvement can actually be dangerous and counterproductive. In a sizable proportion of our study participants, a potentially disquieting trend was developing.

- Those who had an exclusive focus on efficiency were indeed getting more efficient, but they were also becoming increasingly distanced from the real needs of their customers. They were in danger of becoming very good at what they did, but having no idea of what they should actually be good at doing.
- Similarly, those who focused on effectiveness were becoming very good at identifying what their customers needed, but were generally incapable of delivering it fast enough to meet an increased expectation of performance.

It seemed to us that the problems of maintaining a balanced view between efficiency and effectiveness was akin to the problem of climbing to the top of a steep hill. At every point on the trail there are side paths that seem to be easier to take than the direct, but steeper, route to the top. Organizations are tempted to take the side paths, beause they seem to promise gains for less effort. Unfortunately, each deviation from the direct path makes it more of an effort to get back on track later. Figure 3.4 illustrates this problem.

The small number of organizations who were simultaneously pursuing effectiveness and efficiency improvements all commented on the difficulties of maintaining a balanced improvement strategy, along with the continuing temptation to chase apparently easy gains in one direction, at the expense of the other.

Strategic vs. Tactical Improvement Issues

We also observed a practical difficulty in implementing improvement strategies for efficiency, effectiveness, or both. Every one of our study participants commented on a "Catch-22" that they faced. The improvements they wanted to make, while real and possible to implement, took too long to deliver the benefits needed to justify

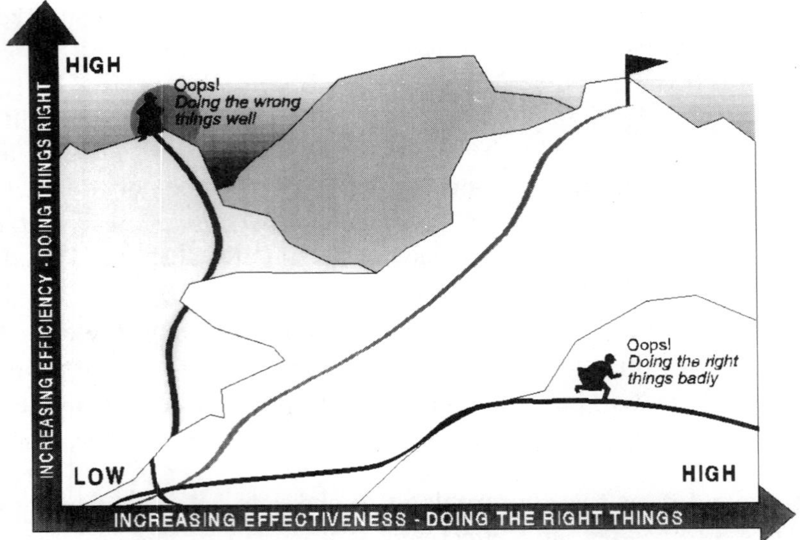

Figure 3.4 *Balancing effectiveness and efficiency targets is a continuing effort.*

the investments required. In general, benefits had to be delivered in less than six months—always in less than a year. However, most improvement programs take from 12 to 30 months to deliver significant and measurable benefits.

As a result, managers of improvement initiatives were all required to look for short-term tactical gains to supplement their longer-term improvement strategies. In many cases, these tactical programs caused a loss of strategic focus, diverting resources into what were, in the end, less than worthwhile efforts. In some instances, organizations lost sight of their strategic objectives in a maze of short-term tactical improvement projects that were individually justifiable, but did not add up to a coherent, self-reinforcing strategic program. Energy got dispersed, enthusiasm and sponsorship waned, and even the tactical benefits were called into doubt.

In addressing these issues with study participants, we determined that the "time to benefit" issue is real, but that there are usually opportunities to finesse the program of tactical actions so that the individual projects remain consistent with longer-term strategic objectives. We call this process "creative cheating." This does not imply unethical behavior on the part of the IS organization—just that the tactical projects must be chosen in such a way that they provide more results faster than might seem to be possible if the projects are examined individually. In particular, nontraditional (nontechnological) leverage opportunities can be used to multiply the effects of tactical projects and create changes that align closely with the desired strategic direction. We will look at a number of these opportunities in the section on acceleration practices.

Getting Past Expectations Based on Past Performance

A commonly recorded comment from most of the IS organizations who were following the effectiveness approach and trying to understand their customers' needs, went something like the following:

> *We're ready and willing to spend time with them [the customers] to find out what they really want—but no one seems to want to spend time with us. Why won't they let us join in? Don't they understand that we want to help them?*

When we went to talk to the customers themselves (not every study participant wanted us to talk with their customers, but most eventually agreed to allow us to do so) we usually got a response that went like this:

> *Why should we spend time talking to them? They were never interested in us before, why should things be any different now? Besides which, we're busy. They don't understand the first thing about how our business works and we don't have*

time to teach them. They can help us best by doing their jobs properly and staying out of our way.

There is an important lesson here, that many IS organizations are slow to learn. You have to earn your place at the table if you want your customers to invest their time in working with you. If you never have been any good (in the customer's eyes) at what you do, why should they have a higher expectation of your performance this time? Getting past this barrier is never easy and takes some up-front investment by the IS organization. In particular:

- The IS organization must learn how to talk with (and not just at) its customers. This means first identifying exactly *who* its customers are, then doing enough homework in advance that a conversation with them is possible. That's an obvious requirement, but not always easy to do. IS organizations have a style and a language that many customers find just about incomprehensible. The IS organization needs to build and practice an effective communications strategy that lets it have a meaningful conversation with business people, on business terms.
- The IS organization needs to come to the table with some immediate and recognizable value. This is where the creative cheating principle comes in again. Find a few low-effort, low-risk, limited-scope, high-reward items that IS can deliver to the business (there are almost always some available). Do a fast, excellent implementation job. Offer the business the results as a reason why closer collaboration pays off ("Look what we were able to do for you once we knew what you needed!"). Develop a low-key but persistent marketing plan for communicating the successes.
- The IS organization needs to establish a basis for value and trust. Too often, the IS organization is a passive order-taker, subject to unmanaged demand from its customers. This makes it difficult to develop and evaluate value prop-

ositions for the work that the IS organization is asked to undertake. It also makes it difficult to track and measure the benefits achieved through the delivery of new or improved information systems. The IS organization needs to start developing effective value propositions that it can use to challenge the appropriateness of the demands placed on it. These value propositions can then form the basis for assessing benefit contribution once the agreed work has been delivered. A key initial step is to identify a small number of *business* measures that all benefits can be tied to. If you claim a contribution to the delivery of a business benefit, it is vital to do so in a way that aligns with how the business measures value. Otherwise your contribution will be devalued or ignored.

- The IS organization needs to understand the characteristics of effective partnerships and how to create them.

One of the reasons that these actions are hard to take is rooted in the culture of IS organizations and their people. In a study of socialization skills among a range of professional groups,[2] IS staff came next to last. Only forest rangers scored lower. This is not such a surprising result. Few IS organizations train their staff in socialization and communication skills, value them if they are operative, or reward their use. Yet forming and operating an effective partnership with customers crucially depend on the availability of such skills on a fairly wide basis. Fortunately, the skills can be taught and most IS staff can learn them.

Focusing on Implementation

In many IS organizations that we studied, it seemed that the pervading culture was "developmental"—focus was on getting devel-

[2]Research conducted by Dr. Robert Zewecki, at the University of Colorado, reported in *Information Week*, July 1994.

opment work completed, with the job considered to be "done" when a new system or a change to an existing system was ready to implement. Significant effort was often put into an "implementation" phase in the development process, but this turned out to be directed at the introduction of the new or changed systems into the IS production environment—a kind of technical implementation only. There was little attention paid, in comparison, to the implementation processes from the customers' point of view.

We saw one very large development project that was scheduled to take 300 people nearly five years to completely "deliver" (that's nearly three million resource hours of development effort). The resulting set of information systems would fundamentally affect the way in which over 12,000 people worked. The first elements of the new system would roll out in year two, with additional elements every few months for three more years. Each roll-out would impact everyone in the target group to some extent. The "field deployment" team was just seven people, and didn't start work until three months before the first roll-out was scheduled to start. Not surprisingly, the customers were soon in revolt, as the scope of the proposed impact became visible. Considerable resources had to be channeled quickly toward "deployment support." This slowed down the development aspects of the project, played havoc with costs and development schedules (every day's delay potentially cost 2,400 staff hours in "wasted" effort), and generally called into question the value of the proposed changes.

In reality, everything in the development process is just preparation—successful implementation in the customers' world is what really counts, because that's where the promised benefits actually start to appear.

Myths That Slow Down the Improvement Process

The Silver Bullet Myth

In *The Mythical Man-Month*,[1] Fred Brooks pointed out that there are no simple, easy-to-implement answers for excellence in software development. He also pointed out that Information Systems (IS) organizations continue to behave as though such easy answers were really available. As each new candidate for the "silver bullet" comes along, it is first "hyped" beyond reason, then embraced without much thought for the consequences, and finally discarded in frustration when it is determined that the fundamental problems remain.

Brooks first described the "Silver Bullet" phenomenon in 1968. I experienced its continuing presence in a group that I addressed as a part of a multi-client research program in the spring of 1994. The group was investigating the difficulties associated with identifying the real information needs of business managers, especially in areas such as competitive intelligence, where the critical information often has relatively little predictable structure. After spending about an hour discussing the difficulties associated with recording a meaningful context for such information, so that it could later be interpreted safely by those who were not involved with its creation, I asked the audience for comments and questions. One of the participants, the CIO for a major division of a telecommunications company, asked "This is all very interesting, but can't you just tell me what to do to solve the problem?"

Nearly as desirable as the single, easy answer, would be a single, difficult answer. But, in most cases, this isn't possible either. We have worked with a number of organizations to help them design and implement improvement programs for their IS organizations. In every instance, we have created improvement programs that contain many related initiatives and actions. The first reaction of the client's management team is always the same: "This is too complicated—give us something simpler."

[1] *The Mythical Man-Month: Essays on Software Engineering*, by Frederick P. Brooks, Jr. Reading, MA: Addison-Wesley, 1982.

It takes considerable time and effort to explain that we have actually made things as simple as possible, yet it still looks uncomfortably complex. Only by walking the IS management team (and sometimes their customers) through the logic of a set of mutually reinforcing, synergistic actions, are we able to persuade them that all of the program components are needed. Only after implementation do they begin to understand how the changes and improvements we seek to create *reinforce* each other, to get the desired levels of improvement. Improvements almost always consist of the cumulative effects of many small but related actions, not just the dramatic impact of a few large ones.

The Universality Myth

When our internal research program first started (in 1989), we were very focused on speed of delivery, which was becoming a significant concern for our practice managers. In general, we were delivering high-quality business solutions to our customers—but it was taking us too long. We wanted to cut our delivery time in half as an initial objective—an aggressive goal[2] that meant that we had to get the new process design right the first time. As a first step in developing an effective improvement strategy, we set out to discover why our process took the time it did.

We "instrumented" a number of our projects with a detailed time-recording system that associated the time spent by the project team members with the deliverables contracted by the project team. As the projects progressed we analyzed the detailed records of time spent, to see how much of the resources being consumed were actually associated with each of the deliverables. We were, to say the least, surprised by what we found.

In our sample of projects (all of which were considered to be "well managed" and successful) only 45 percent of the total re-

[2]Interestingly enough, this goal should not require innovation—just extensive improvement in the underlying processes.

sources consumed by the project could be directly associated with the deliverables produced by the project. This was a "fully burdened" percentage, taking into account necessary project-management tasks and required administration overheads, as well as directly attributed effort. This was such an unexpectedly low result that we immediately suspected that either our research methodology or our data-capture tool was at fault. As we followed-up the results with interviews with the project teams, however, a different pattern emerged.

First, there were two sources of genuine attributable effort that did not show up in our resource-attributed-to-deliverable analysis:

- **Effort required by the problem-discovery process.** When identifying a business problem, project teams had all spent time looking in places where the problem *was not*, in order to be sure that they had correctly identified the place where the problem actually *was*. This was real and necessary effort, but did not generally get recorded against a deliverable.
- **Effort required to develop and analyze solution options that were not, in the event, actually used.** Once the problem had been correctly identified, project teams had a number of possible solutions available to them, only one of which was actually implemented. Effort was required to develop the basis for a rational selection among the possibilities for a solution. Once again, this effort was not generally recorded against a deliverable.

The combined effect of these two findings was to account for about 20 percent of the total project effort, taking our "valid resource consumption" total to around 65 percent. But that was the limit to what we could account for. So where did the remaining 35 percent of our consumed resources go? Here again, our follow-up analysis was interesting and surprising. We discovered three principal explanations for this "lost" effort.

1. Many of the people staffing the project did not really understand *why* they were doing what they were doing—even though they generally knew *how* to do the work that they were assigned to do. They did know, however, that they would be measured by how busy they were—by their utilization. Not surprisingly, therefore, they tended to do as much of their assigned work as they could—whether or not it was needed. This lack of a "big picture" view of the project was very common.
2. There was a substantial amount of effort expended to correct problems resulting from "defects" that entered the process at some earlier stage. Many of these defects resulted from missing or poorly articulated requirements. This is a key issue, and will be discussed a little later in this section.
3. Effort was being expended on work that was required, in general, by the development process being used, but which was actually not required for the particular project being undertaken. In other words, some of the work in the plan was required by some projects, but not by all projects. However, because the project team had no guidelines on when to exclude or include the work, they tended to include it, just in case.

We discovered that the most common reason for the third type of lost effort (and a fairly common cause related to the first) was the use of a standard development methodology. Methodologies tended to treat every project as if it was the same, whereas in practice, every instance of a project is, to some degree, different. By treating every project the same, methodologies drove project planners to create work plans that contained work that was unnecessary, or not value-added, for a particular project. Project teams faced with work plans that they did not fully understand, but with utilization measures very much in mind, worked the plan. The results? Virtually all of the 35 percent of well-intentioned effort for no useful result was now explained. If we could get this 35 percent back, we would be well on our way to achieving the 50 percent reduction in cycle time that was our target.

Eight Dimensions of Variability

If every project is, to some degree, different, what are the characteristics or factors that determine these differences? This is a hard question to answer with confidence. The more sources of variability you suspect, the more sets of project data you need to test whether a particular source has a measurable, and therefore predictable, effect. We could readily list dozens of potential sources of variability, but we had only a few hundred data sets for analysis. This detailed analytic approach was interesting but, without a lot more data, it was not going to get us very far. In the end, we grouped our suspected sources of variability into eight "dimensions" that seemed to account for most of the differences that mattered to us. These were:

1. **The characteristics of the problem domain.** This dimension lets us factor-in differences due to the type, scale, scope, or complexity of the business problem we are trying to address. We can also account for differences due to situational variables, such as industry, market, company culture, organization structure, and so on.
2. **The characteristics of the solution domain.** This dimension lets us look at factors associated with the type, scale, scope, and complexity of the proposed solution that we want to develop. We can also factor in variables related to how new or *different* the solution is from the current state.
3. **The approach to be taken to identify the problem and create a solution.** This lets us account for differences that arise from *how* we execute the work plan, rather than just the work content (*what* we plan to do). It also lets us deal with factors that determine how difficult some aspects of the work are to execute correctly.

4. **The skills and experience of the project team.** This is an obvious factor, but a critical one, since the performance capabilities of experienced staff often differ radically from those of less-experienced staff. This is especially important for projects that will use new or unfamiliar technologies, and is an area that we will look at in more detail later.
5. **The tools and techniques used to support the solution-development process.** We don't always get to use the tools we want, so we need to assess factors that are related to how well the tools we have available match the needs of the job they support.
6. **The target technology environment for the solution.** This dimension lets us deal with factors such as infrastructure stability, the use of new, unfamiliar or unproved technologies, integration requirements, capacity issues, and so on.
7. **The baseline knowledge available at the start of the project.** This is important. One of the major sources of wasted effort that we identified was discovery work on information that was already known when the project started, but was *not* known to the project team.
8. **The selected implementation approach for the solution.** This factor has a subtle but often crucial effect. Some implementation strategies require preparatory work to begin much earlier than others, and the project planners must take this into account.

There are some important points to note. First, this is clearly not a rigorous taxonomy. The dimensions are not really orthogonal (independent of each other), so they do not really combine as matrix products.

Second, even if the dimensions were independent, the space defining all projects generated from the algebraic combination of the eight dimensions is sparse—many of the projects that we could describe using this combinatorial approach are not feasible for a variety of reasons that are not part of the characterization model (we call these variables exogenous—meaning resulting from the outside). Just figuring the most likely domain sizes for the eight dimensions, however, gives us in excess of 100 billion feasible combinations for possible projects—many more than we could ever actually do.

Third, each of the dimensions is really a multivariate combination of factors, and we have not attempted a rigorous factor analysis to confirm what the correct combinations of component variables should be. As a result, this is really just a way to collect characteristics of projects in a systematic way, so that we can attempt to use sources of variability analysis to develop the basis for a first-order optimization of the work plan.

Finally, this is not supposed to be an exhaustive set of sources of variability in development projects. Nor would we claim that all sources of variability can, in some way, be mapped to one of the eight dimensions listed here. Nevertheless, most of the variations we have seen in the several hundred projects that we have now analyzed can be explained using these sets of characterizing variables.

Optimization through Specialization

Once we established the project characteristics model, we started to use it to influence the way in which projects were planned. Initially we used two research approaches:

1. We took a few (about 20 out of 300) of the already-completed projects for which we had the original work plans and planning assumptions in machine-readable form, and looked at the differences in resource estimates that would have resulted if they had been planned using the characeristics model. It turned out that these projects would have been, on average, 28% smaller when they were planned, if all factors known to the project planners were taken into account. The absolute range was from 11 percent to 43 percent. None of them would have been larger. This gave us a quick verification that we were on the right track.

2. We began to plan new projects using the characterization approach. Every project was also planned using the old (unspecialized) approach. We had a larger sample population to work with here (we had access to several hundred projects in the first year) but we would obviously have to wait until the projects actually finished to get outcome data, and we could not fully duplicate the planning and estimation effort for every project to the degree we would have wished.

This time, we got slightly different improvement results. The projects were still mostly smaller in terms of planned resources, but only by 20 percent, on average. We also got a small percentage (about 4 percent) of projects that had *larger* resource estimates using the characterization approach than without it. The absolute range was from 17 percent larger to 34 percent smaller. Given the small size of the initial sample that we tested retroactively, the 8 percent difference between the two results may not be statistically significant, but it looked like it should be and, in any case, the variation in range was disturbing.

Closer examination of the outlying values in the second group all showed some degree of poor estimation assumptions, or related misunderstandings of requirements by the estimators, and we were able to eliminate these from the sample. This gave us a recalculated average of 24 percent smaller and a range of 13 percent to 34 percent smaller. So why are the specialized project estimates smaller, and does a reduced resource estimate translate to a smaller outcome?

The resource estimates are smaller because the project plans for the specialized projects were able to eliminate "generic" work for which unspecialized estimates would have been used, and replace it with specialized work for which more granular estimates could be arrived at. As a by-product of this work, we built a suite of automated tools that assisted project planners to implement the specialization process. These tools did not change the size of the projects that were planned using them, but they did reduce the time required to create a specialized plan from more than 40 hours to less than four.

Smaller estimates do indeed translate into smaller outcomes. As the projects planned using our new process were completed, we collected and analyzed the actual resources required to complete them. Of course, we did not actually *do* the projects twice, so it could be argued that we don't know what would have happened if the projects had been run using the unspecialized plans. What we did do was compare the outcomes with projects from our original research database, getting as close a match as possible for the characteristics. Since we do a lot of the same kinds of projects, this was possible, if not completely rigorous.

What we found was an average of 16 percent reduced resources at completion. The absolute range was 3 percent to 22 percent. Just by modifying the project-planning process, we were able to get back almost half of the 35 percent of "wasted" resources that we were chasing. This was a fairly good result, but why didn't we get all of the initial improvements to be reflected in the project outcomes? What caused the relatively large differences? Our follow-up analysis identified a number of sources of the "loss":

- **Overoptimism in planning and estimating assumptions.** Although no individual assumption was unreasonable, the set of assumptions, taken as a whole, added up to way too optimistic a view of what would probably happen. In essence, project planners correctly identified most of the things that could go wrong with the project, but then assumed that few or none of them would actually happen. Surprisingly, even experienced project managers, who you would think would know better, who used their experience to verify the sources of risk exhibited this overoptimism.
- **Surfacing unanticipated requirements.** Here, the discovery process had turned up a significant number of essential requirements that had not been anticipated

when the project was planned. Meeting these exceeded the contingency that had been provided. This situation was most prevalent in projects that were significantly changing the operation of current state processes and the requirements were often related to integration issues with existing information systems.

- **Other types of unplanned work.** After the first two causes, there were a whole host of less-well-defined sources of unplanned work that resulted in expansion of the original estimates. These included: unavoidable but unplanned staff substitutes during the project (for many reasons), and unexpected unavailability of key resources; infrastructure availability delays and technology stability problems, resulting from version updates to components; development tool failures; and sponsorship changes.

We rediscovered in our analysis what we really had already conceded: we don't (and can't) anticipate all sources of variability of outcome in advance. But that's no excuse for not trying, or for not being a lot smarter about how we plan and estimate work.

The Completeness Myth

Our next stop on the mythology trail concerns the very common IS trait of overengineering solutions. In many projects, the deliverables that were being produced were far more elaborate than really required. We saw instances where over 20 percent of total resources were consumed "polishing the deliverables." When we asked the project teams why they spent so much time "improving" what were already complete project outputs, we almost always got the "quality matters to us and our customers" response. That's fine, but when we asked the customers if they appreciated the extra effort being expended on their behalf, most said something like:

> *Well, now that you ask, we wondered why the project team spent so much time on those sorts of things. We were quite happy with their first or second attempt. They could have stopped then and moved on. We assumed that all the extra work was for their benefit—it didn't make any difference to us. Although, now that you mention it, it did seem to slow things down.*

So, if the deliverable didn't need it, and the customers didn't want it, what did "quality matters" have to do with it?

Productivity and Quality Issues

Notice that we are not condoning or suggesting the delivery of poor, unfinished, or inappropriate work. Instead, we suggest that the IS organization and its project teams develop an understanding of the customer's desired levels of quality. Have this agreement *before* the project starts, so that if the customer expects a pickup truck, they will get a really good pickup truck—not a Cadillac. Most customers won't turn down the Cadillac when it's offered, but they will probably wonder why you built them one, and they may want it at the price of a pickup.

We saw a great example of this in two projects undertaken by the U.S.-based and U.K.-based IS groups from a well-known fast-food company. Both groups needed to develop an improved touch-sensitive terminal for use by the order-takers in their retail outlets. It had to be very easy to use (fast-food servers are not necessarily technology literate and they don't get a lot of technology training), cheap to build (many would be needed), safe (lots of children on the order-giving side), and durable (this is the fast-food industry, and spills are a fact of life). Sound like a "pickup" to you?

Both groups built prototypes, which were generally similar, worked fine, and passed an initial field test. One group then spent a year refining and "improving" their prototype until it was complicated to operate, expensive to build, and too fragile. It became more like a sophisticated sports car than a pickup.

The other group spent a month creating a production version of their prototype, quickly installed it in many outlets, and started a low-key continuous-improvement program based on user feedback. Their answer was cheap, easy to operate, safe, and reliable. They'd built a great "pickup."

Which group do you think won out in the end? The "sports car," of course. It was the "quality solution." They're still trying to figure out how to afford it.

The important rule here is just another manifestation of the Pareto principle: 80 percent of the value is realized from 20 percent of the solution—and there is no value at all until you implement something that real business people can use in real business situations. Getting the *right* first 20 percent developed and into use is the best way to be successful. You will still end up delivering the remaining 80 percent in some form, but it will probably not be what you planned at the outset. Once the customers have used the facilities represented by the first 20 percent of the solution, their perception of what they need next will change.

Your customers' new perception will define the next most important 20 percent, and so on, through many incremental iterations. Of course, this requires us to abandon many of our ideas about what "finished" means and to learn to tolerate the percentage of our work that will be discarded as our customers' awareness grows.

This approach has a great deal of power, but also has some difficult problems that complicate its use. Firstly, you can't choose just any 20 percent of the total requirements. There are critical dependencies in any business process design that must be recognized by the systems that support it. These dependencies determine the boundaries for feasible systems projects and are difficult or impossible to ignore. Figuring them out takes specialized business knowledge.

Second, there are technology dependencies that have to be accounted for in the infrastructure that support the changed elements of the business process. Figuring these out takes specialized technology knowledge.

Third, there are integration constraints imposed by the parts of the business process that won't initially be changed and by other business processes that are linked to the process we are changing in various ways. If we can't decouple these constraints in an effective way, we may not get enough benefit from the 20 percent we have selected. If we can't identify the constraints, we can't attempt to decouple them. Figuring out the constraints takes both business and technology knowledge. Figure 4.1 shows an example of why this is an issue.

Over time, business processes and the systems that support them can become hopelessly entangled as enhancements and modifications to the initial (hopefully straightforward) architecture are added. This makes the interfacing effort and cost prohibitive for

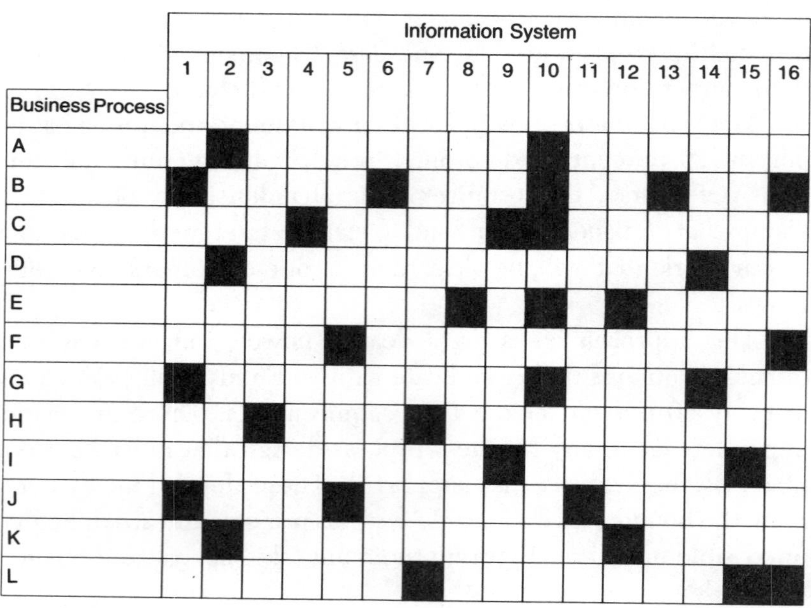

Figure 4.1 *The complex interconnections of current-state systems and processes can prevent the definition of small project boundaries.*

some otherwise viable projects. When these situations occur, the smallest economically viable project may be much bigger than 20 percent of the total requirements.

The Management Myth

In high-performing organizations, management is mostly about coordination and communication. Coordination and communication within organizations can generally be accomplished by any one of three broad categories of mechanisms:

1. **Mutual adjustment.** Work is under the control of those who carry it out. The process of informal communication is used to coordinate work. Workers perform their tasks and, as needed, contact other workers, who then adjust to the new information. Self-directed work groups or teams are an example of this mechanism.
2. **Direct supervision.** Work is under the control of a supervisor. One individual takes responsibility for the assignments of others. Communication is fed downward through instructions or orders and upward via results and status reports. The military chain of command is a classic example of direct supervision.
3. **Standardization.** Work is under the control of predetermined specifications, of which there are generally three types:

   - Standardization of work processes.
   - Standardization of deliverables or work outputs.
   - Standardization of skills or work content.

   Coordination of work is accomplished by everyone following exacting guidelines on what to do, what to produce, and/or how to produce it. The production-line manufacturing process commonly uses some form of this mechanism.

Most organizations tend to favor one coordinating mechanism over the others, but no organization can rely, long term, on only one such mechanism to communicate and coordinate all types of work effectively. Many IS organizations tend to favor the direct supervision approach, with occasional (but regular) attempts at standardization, using methodologies or specific training programs. To some extent, all three coordinating mechanisms are necessary. However, each type has its values and drawbacks. Each is also suited to address a specific range of problem types.

Take a look at Figure 4.2. When problems are simple, using a *mutual adjustment* approach to coordinate and communicate makes good sense and works effectively.

The process used to solve simple problems is usually self-evident and requires little, if any, structure or elaboration between co-workers. However, when the problems begin to get more com-

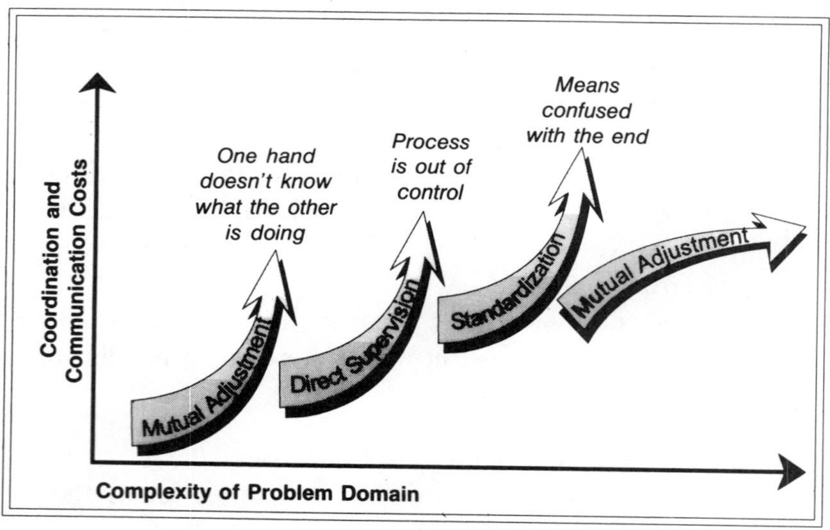

Figure 4.2 *Different coordination and communication mechanisms should be used for increasingly complex problem domains.*

plex, the coordination costs for mutual adjustment rise exponentially. A minor example of this can be seen from the actions of the little girl who received conflicting commands from her two coaches. The more complex, or less standardized, the work, the less clear it is *who is responsible* for doing *what* when only a mutual adjustment coordinating mechanism is used. Eventually a communications barrier develops that can prevent more complex problems from being solved.

At this point, most organizations try to impose order and accountability. *Direct supervision* fills the bill by having one person take responsibility for the work of others. This hierarchy provides structure around the assignment of tasks, and allows a new class of more complex problems to be solved—albeit at the price of additional coordination costs, because a direct supervisor often plays no part in carrying out the work being supervised.

Direct supervision also seems to run into a barrier when it comes to handling even more complex problems. As tasks handed down from supervisors become more complex, the process needed to identify, perform, and complete the tasks becomes harder for those doing the work. Eventually the supervisors have to ask workers to perform tasks that they themselves cannot perform and for which they therefore cannot provide direct guidance. Workers are forced to invent a process each time they receive a new task. Work quickly becomes unpredictable in execution and unreliable in output. Adding either additional resources or additional supervision—or both—only makes things worse. The work process is perceived to be out of control.

It has been said that research anthropologists working in the 1950s attributed this "failure of group supervision" phenomenon to the early evolutionary history of human beings. Their theory proposed that the maximum size of an effective supervised group was approximately equal to the maximum practical size of a Neolithic hunting party (typically 10 to 15 people). If the group is smaller than this, the prey just as often gets the hunters. Larger parties make too much noise; thus too much of the game gets scared away, and some of the hunters starve. The anthropologists believed that humans have yet to evolve beyond this environmental constraint on group behavior.

To solve problems of greater complexity, many organizations have turned to *standardization*, instead of increased supervision, as a coordinating mechanism. Through standardizing work processes, outputs, or the skills believed to be necessary to do the work, the process to produce deliverables is brought under control and a new class of more complex problems can be solved, also at the cost of additional coordination effort. Mass-production, or assembly-line processes often use standardization effectively. The process of constructing a product from a good design can be standardized to reduce variability and to serve as a platform upon which to improve.

However, like the other coordinating mechanisms, standardization encounters a limit to the complexity of the problems it can address effectively. Problems that take a very long time to solve, or have never before been solved, are difficult targets for standards. People often faithfully adhere to a known process without acknowledging the failure of the process to solve a new or more complex problem. In other words, the means become confused with the ends.

For very complex problems, or problems that have not been solved before, an organization must return, paradoxically, to a mutual adjustment form of coordination. Sophisticated problem-solvers almost always communicate informally. Innovative design processes require some form of mutual adjustment. When a manufacturer is designing a new product, exactly what needs to be done at the outset is not known. The knowledge develops as the work unfolds. The success of the overall effort depends on the ability of various experts to adapt knowledge, behavior, and beliefs to one another along an uncharted route.

This model is based on the principle that each time a problem is solved, the next time the same or similar problem arises it is considered, to some extent, to be less complex than it was before. This will be true only if an organization has an effective way to capture and codify experience and to communicate the results to workers who did not gain the experience directly.

The "More Must Be Better" Myth

As our research data sets built up, we continued to look for ways to reduce cycle times in parts of the development process. One area where we were spending a lot of time and resources was "requirements analysis"—the early stages of the project where we were still focused on identifying and documenting our customers' needs. One of the principal reasons for paying a lot of attention to requirements stemmed from our adoption, over a five-year period starting in the mid-1980s, of the underlying principles of Information Engineering (IE), based on the ideas of James Martin[3] and others.

IE-based approaches recognize that many of the rework problems that are encountered in the design and development of information systems stem from process failures during requirements analysis. If we can get the requirement analysis right, therefore, these sources of rework will be eliminated. There is substantial research to support the basic observation that underlies this thesis, but when we put the principles into practice, we saw large increases in the resource cost and elapsed time for requirements analysis, without a corresponding decrease in later rework. We were seeing a lot more requirements analysis, but we were not seeing better requirements.

It seemed that, not only were we not very good at doing requirements analysis, we were also spending a larger proportion of time and resources on it. If, no matter how hard you try, you can't do something well, you should be trying to do *less* of it, not more. What should we be doing instead?

The first impulse on seeing this situation is to blame the phe-

[3] *Information Engineering*, Volumes 1–4, by James Martin. Englewood Cliffs, NJ: Prentice-Hall, 1987.

nomenon on the quality of the staff on the requirements-analysis team. We couldn't really accept this as the explanation, since the staff working on the requirements phase of a project are usually among our best and most experienced people. If these folks were really the source of the problem, our whole hiring, staff development, and training process must be badly broken and we did not believe that it was. We needed a better explanation.

Our initial analysis looked at the correlation between the effort put into requirements analysis and the quality of the resulting requirements. We defined requirements quality in terms of the number of changes that were required during the design and development phases of a project and the degree of customer satisfaction after implementation of the project's deliverables. We looked, in particular, at the 25 percent or so of projects which had both high customer satisfaction scores and low change rates to see how much requirements analysis had been done. We discovered something very interesting, and more than a little alarming. There was no correlation between the amount of effort that went into requirements analysis and the quality of the requirements that resulted from the work. When we tested this result on the complete population of projects, we discovered the same thing. Finally, we tried it on the "worst" 25 percent of projects that had low customer satisfaction scores and high change rates. The finding remained exactly the same.

These results caused us to take a fundamental look at what was going on in requirements analysis and to reexamine our data to see if there was a correlation that might explain why we got better results on some projects than on others. When we reanalyzed the best 25 percent of projects, we discovered that all of them had shown their customers examples and prototypes that were close, in look, feel, and behavior, to the finished application. Even more interesting was the fact that they had begun this process very early on in requirements analysis. In essence, they were using examples and prototypes, usually developed elsewhere, to identify and confirm requirements.

Once we had this clue, we tested the hypothesis that there should be a link between requirements quality and early exposure to something close to the final solution. Not surprisingly, the correlation was clearly present in the complete data set. Projects that had not used prototyping or best-practice examples during requirements analysis scored poorly on requirements quality. Projects that did use prototypes, but that did not manage to create a prototype that was close to the final solution, also fared poorly.

In seeking an explanation for these results, we formed the conclusion that requirements analysis is not just, or even mostly about analyzing requirements using the classic "find the problem, then solve it" model that we (and virtually everyone else) had been using. Instead, requirements analysis is mostly *about mutual education* between customers and IS developers, building confidence that both sets of participants understands the needs, capabilities, and constraints of the other.

This is why we can't draw the obvious corollary from our initial findings: that no requirements analysis is just as good as a lot of requirements analysis, and very much cheaper, so we might as well abandon requirements analysis altogether. Instead, we should seek to design a requirements-capture process that recognizes the nature of a successful mutual education experience. Then we can manage to the needs of the process, instead of to an abstract model of objectives that, however rational, had turned out to be unworkable.

A final word on requirements capture. One of the most powerful ideas in effective requirements analysis is rapid iteration—creating a series of requirements statements and resulting solutions that converge to an agreed final solution. Each step in the series takes the requirements team back to the beginning of the process, but provides a richer and better informed starting point. After a few iterations, the answer isn't getting any better, so we move on to build the solution and implement it.

We have been using this approach for many years, generally with very good results, but we have had a few instances (and observed many more) that degenerated into "requirements thrashing." Here the iterations do not converge to an agreed solution. Instead, the requirements process repeats endlessly until patience or budgets run out, victory is declared, and we move on.

There are many possible reasons for these failures (the wrong problem, the wrong people, and a badly managed issue resolution process are frequent causes), but one very common cause is the lack of easy-to-use stopping rules—definitions of conditions that you can test for and stop if they are present. At various times we have developed and attempted to operationalize sophisticated stopping rules for projects that took many factors into account. Most of these attempts failed, not because the rules were no good—they actually worked just fine—but because they never got applied. Our rules were too complicated for our project teams to use reliably. So we came up with a much simpler rule, based on our empirical analysis of high-quality-requirements projects, for controlling iteration. We call it "*the stop after three rule*" and it recognizes the fact that requirements do not get enough better after three iterations to justify the cost of a fourth. After three cycles, go and build the result. Doing that may get you a better answer, where more analysis will not.

The "We Know What We Want" Myth

About ten years ago I read a magazine column in which the author questioned the enormous price difference between *dBase III* and *IDMS* database-management products. *IDMS*, a sophisticated, large volume database-management system for mainframe computers, was about a thousand times more expensive than *dBase III*, a useful but small-scale product for personal computers. To Pournelle, who actually used *dBase*, but not *IDMS*, they were equivalent—both managed files of data.

In fact, *dBase* was usable only by a single person, maintained only a single access path into the data, had no real transaction security, and only rudimentary management tools. *IDMS* allowed data to be shared between hundreds of users at the same time, allowed many access paths, provided transaction security, and powerful management tools. These differences made no difference to Pournelle, so he did not value them.

Herein lies the dangers of a little technical knowledge among the IS organization's customers. Over the last ten years I have seen many similar arguments put forward, but they were usually in IT-oriented publications. More recently, there has also been a trend to present technology matters in mainstream business publications. Some recent examples include *Business Week* articles on Object-Oriented Programming,[4] Neural Networks[5] and the Internet.[6,7] Similar articles have appeared in *Fortune* magazine.[8]

These articles are usually well researched and well written, but they target a non-technical business audience and must necessarily lack much in the way of technical depth. As awareness-building vehicles, they do a competent job of describing complex technologies in straightforward terms. Yet I know many CIOs who dread them.

Why? Because the articles leave out all the hard parts that take time and background to explain. They create the impression, whether or not they set out to do so, that the technologies they describe are readily available and mature; that they are easy to use; that just about everyone is already using them, and if *your* company is not, you are missing the boat.

So what happens? The next day in comes an irate CEO, or CFO, or COO, or VP of manufacturing, or whatever, demanding to know when XYZ Inc. will be using object-oriented programming to develop neural agents to do business over the Internet, and "Why aren't we already doing it? Isn't that what we pay you IS guys for?"

Add in another recent phenomenon. As PCs have gotten cheaper and cheaper, many executives who don't have PCs at work, *do* have them at home. They use extremely sophisticated and very

[4] *Business Week*, September 30, 1991, pp. 58–63.
[5] *Business Week*, July 12, 1994, pp. 190–193.
[6] *Business Week*, November 14, 1994, pp. 80–88.
[7] *Business Week*, February 27, 1995, pp. 78–88.
[8] Managing in a wired world, *Fortune*, July 11, 1994, pp. 44–115.

cheap software (such as word processors and graphics programs) that support color, have instant tutorials, and provide "Wizards" for the hard parts.[9] The software is also, relatively, bug-free.

This is the application benchmark that they come to expect from *all* the applications they use. They have the Jerry Pournelle perspective—they never experience the problems of scaling up single-user experience to the corporate environment. But they certainly know that they want their large-scale business software to look, feel, and behave just like the great products they use at home.

We are also seeing a related phenomenon growing from the popularizing of information technology among business executives. Increasingly, business managers are showing up at the IS organizations doorstep with technology that they have bought that they want the IS folks to make work. It doesn't matter that their new toys are non-standard, don't integrate with any existing infrastructure, and require specialized skills that are in short supply. It also doesn't seem to matter that there is often no business problem for which the new technology is a solution. The IS organization has to find something to do with it anyway.

Difficult though this situation is, smart IS organizations can use the growing technological literacy among their customers to their advantage, if they are prepared to change their own processes to respond to it. Instead of traditional requirements-capture methods ("tell me what you want"), substitute "best of breed" product comparisons and technology demonstrations to surface and define improvement opportunities. If your customers are going to get exposed to this "pop" technology anyway, get ahead of them and establish the IS organization as a reliable source of news about new technology and the things that can really be done with it.

[9] Microsoft's *Excel* spreadsheet package, which can be bought for under $100, represents about 5,000 function points of content. That's about the same as a medium-sized business application. Microsoft can sell it for two cents retail, a function point, because they will sell millions of copies. Most users will only touch about 10% of the available functionality, but for under $100, who cares? The IS organization will build only a few copies of applications software and even a few thousand is too few to get Microsoft's economies of scale.

We saw a good example of this at one of the world's largest engineering project-management companies. The corporate IS group had spent years building a "new generation" project management support system that tied together the ccompany's other information systems and maximized the effectiveness of engineering and project managers in bidding and then running projects. Unfortunately their solution kept getting blind-sided by new technology that was readily available and relatively cheap (in the context of a $500 million project, even $25,000 is "cheap"). Nevertheless, they kept going, always asking "OK, what do you want next?" Their system actually made it into use on a few projects.

Meanwhile, the IS group supporting the new business acquisition process had built up a much less monolithic answer for estimating and bidding for contracts, based on familiar components that the engineerings and project managers found easy to use because they worked just like the software they used at home. As new features made it into the retail software marketplace they were quickly incorporated into the business support software. No one felt left behind by technology.

When it came time to radically re-engineer the bidding and proposal process, the small-scale familiar answer was chosen as the basis to go forward. Not because it was "better" or more complete (it was neither) but because everyone knew how to use it.

The "We Know What You Want" Myth

Of course, the IS organization is hardly blame-free in providing solutions in search of problems. This is especially true in two common scenarios:

1. The IS organization invests heavily in a new technology without first establishing that it is a good match to the business-process requirements of the enterprise it sup-

ports. It must then justify the investment by retrofitting the technology to the needs (best case) or the needs to the technology (worst case). This situation can arise even when there is a regular dialog with customers.

2. The IS organization never talks to its customers about anything, so whatever it does, even if it creates good answers to business problems, will be treated with suspicion and probably resisted.

Where technology leads the solution-identification process, but is not being used to leverage process innovation, there is a danger that the solutions that are created will either not work, or, if they do work, will be much more expensive to use than they needed to be. Of course, the temptation is to claim that this scenario is really technology-led innovation—but that's hardly ever the case.

The Methodology Myth

I have a long list of the things that I dislike about existing IS development methods (including some methods that I have been responsible for developing). Out of this list, a few things stand out:

Audience

It always seems to me that methodology is built primarily for methodologists—not for the practitioners who will have to use it on real-world projects. As a result, most methodologies have characteristics that make them unnecessarily difficult to deploy effectively. For example:

- **Uniform expectations of competence.** No account is taken of variations in ability and experience in the target audience. Everyone is expected to be equally good at doing everything described in the methodology (and often at doing things that are not described but necessary, anyway).

- **Accelerating change and the accumulation of relevant experience.** As more new development technologies and corresponding implementation platforms are introduced, the amount that any one practitioner needs to know to perform well also increases. As a result, specialization tends to occur. Methodologies take little or no account of this.
- **The identification of different "target" practitioners.** As a result, there are usually several different target groups of practitioners who will perform different roles but who must collaborate in a common framework to get the application built and delivered. Help on how to identify and assign relevant roles and how to steer practitioners toward appropriate roles on a project is usually missing.

These are, however, relatively easy aspects to address.

Failures in Concept

More serious are the issues associated with the way that methodologies support the model of a project and the organization of work within it.

- **Technological focus obscures business needs.** Methodologies are too often focused on the use of the technologies available to the IS organization and too little on the rapid and accurate identification of business problems and how to solve them well. A good test is to see if there is a way to solve a problem *without* any information technology in the solution. Since problems like this really do exist and the IS organization will definitely face them from time to time, it should be possible to get an appropriate nontechnological answer. If it isn't possible, customers should beware of the solutions they are being offered.

- **The development of information systems requires more than just analysis and design.** Methodologies seldom have much to say about anything except requirements analysis and system design. What gets left out (strategy at the start of the life cycle, and construction and implementation at the end) is just as important to achieving a good business solution. And no one seems to want to talk about "maintenance" at all, even though it's most of what we all do and represents 80 to 90 percent of the ownership costs of software.
- **Every project seems to be the same.** Every project seems to be treated the same way irrespective of its type scope, size, objectives, and technical environment. In practice, this is unreasonably simplistic. We should recognize the effects of at least the most common critical factors.
- **Yesterday's problems.** It is almost inevitable that methodologies look toward the past. After all, they are built from experience that occurred in the past. Yet they are often used to solve problems that are new, occurring only in the present. We would also want to be able to solve problems we have not yet experienced, problems that will occur in the future.
- **Cosmetics.** It often seems to be more important to remember what a deliverable is supposed to look like than to understand what it's for (particularly to that strange group of practitioners concerned with the accreditation of tools to support some public domain methods).
- **Every task is presented as equally easy (or equally hard).** Few methodologies distinguish between the tasks that are easy to do well and the ones that are hard, or require specific experience or competency. If you don't have this information available, how can you make rational work assignments? Or assign work to staff so that it will help them develop or extend their skills?

- **Nothing ever goes wrong.** Everything in a project is assumed to be perfect and nothing ever seems to go wrong, so there is no advice on what to do when problems occur or when things can't be done in the order suggested (or enforced) by the method. A good methodology should at least provide hints on avoidance, problem diagnostics, and recovery strategies.

Failures in Process

Finally, there are failures related to the processes that methodologies make us use to design the projects that we must undertake.

- **Justifying the work.** There is too much emphasis on a work breakdown structure and too little on deliverables and on the work actually required to create and validate them effectively. Methods make us do too many things that don't contribute much or anything to the real deliverable from a development project—a working application. It should be possible to justify every activity in a project in terms of its contribution to this objective, and all too often it isn't. Too often we have no way of knowing what must be included and what can be safely left out.
- **Evolution.** It's always assumed that a project starts with essentially a clean sheet of paper—an empty repository in today's terms. This will seldom be true in future development environments, where the repository will almost always contain some or all of the components required for any new development project as a result of past development or enhancement efforts.

Methodologies are still a good idea. In theory they are essential to a sustained, high-performance software-development capability. But too many of those that have been developed in the past fail to do the job that is really needed.

The "We Are Different" Myth

In 1987 I was invited to speak (about a process for developing methodologies) at a conference in Cambridge, England, organized by the British Computer Society (BCS). One of the other invited speakers was Michael Jackson, who pioneered many of the structured design and coding schemes that we use to write program code today. Part of his topic, on efficient program design strategies, related to the need for justification for the actual code of a program—in essence, the ability to say why a particular instruction was present in the code. Jackson called this "genotyping" the code. This idea struck me at the time as more than just an interesting approach to provide insight into program structure analysis. Over the intervening years, I have tried to apply this principle to the various kinds of software that I have built or for which I have managed the development. As a result, I have built up a collection of analyses of the executing image of various types of software, that allows the "origin" of the code to be recorded. While this does not approach the individual instruction granularity of Jackson's genotyping proposal, it has allowed me to identify and record the source of the many different components that make up a modern software application. This structural analysis also helps to answer three other related questions:

- How much actual influence do we have, as developers, over the code that makes up our applications?
- How much of the proportion of code that we *can* influence *should* we care about?
- How much of what we *should* be doing are we *actually* doing when we develop application software?

The execution image of a modern business process support application is enormous—typically several megabytes of object code, plus tens of megabytes of related components. It will include components from many different sources, including "local" developers. The image is generally much bigger than it was prior to the introduction of graphical user interfaces and distributed data architectures, but the distribution of the code has remained remarkably stable. Table 4.1 summarizes the results of my analysis of several thousand application images developed to run on a fairly wide range of target technology platforms.

The profile that results is remarkably independent of the actual technologies used. Although the specific values do vary somewhat, the line between what we can influence as developers (the answer to the first of our three questions) and what we cannot, is fairly well fixed at about 35 percent (plus or minus about 3 percent), no matter what combination of hardware, operating system, database manager, transaction manager, and development language we

Table 4.1 *Summarized Structural Analysis of Applications Software*

Origin of Code in Executing Application Image	Percent
Operating system supplied services and system utilities	22
Data communications, networking and transaction management, including concurrency control, transaction recovery, and commit logic	13
Data management, including standard data access, data, and view synchronization and metadata management	15
User interface behavior, interface control, data presentation, and interaction management	15
Industry or market-wide business rules and inter-enterprise process and data structure definition conventions, including regulatory requirements and conventions	15
Enterprise-wide business rules and process or data structure definition conventions	15
Problem-specific rules, processing logic, or data structure definitions	5

choose. There are some extreme values in the sample, but they are not in the mainstream of commercial application development platforms and technologies. Therefore I have eliminated them from the summarized data.

What is the logical target for our developers? Build only the 5 percent or so of the application that consists of problem-specific logic (that's the first answer to our second question). We should be able to build everything else just once, or get it from somewhere or someone who has already developed, tested, and published it. This is the ultimate target of the component-reuse model. We might even be able to use common components from the problem-specific set in multiple problems, since we actually deal with a fairly small set of possible processing actions, business rules, and logical requirements. In this case we could get the new coding down to perhaps 1 percent or 2 percent of the total image. That could still be a megabyte or two of code, but it's a lot less work than developing the 50 to 100 megabytes of the whole application.

Even if we don't have any of the common industry and enterprise components available, we should still never have to build more than 35 percent of an application (that's the second answer to our second question).

So, if 35 percent of the execution image is the maximum we actually *need* to develop from scratch, what's the average proportion that we actually *do* develop? I don't have these data explicitly for every program I've collected, so some of the attributions are judgmental, but even allowing for this factor, the answer is a surprising 45 percent. On average we develop *ten percent more* of the total execution image of an application than the maximum we actually *need* to. Why do we do this? Most of the reasons we could identify can be summed up quite simply: *inexperienced or undertrained developers.* You have to know enough to be good at a lot of different things to develop modern business software applications, and many developers *do not know* everything they need to know about all of the topics they need. As a result, they develop code that was already available from some other source, or they don't trust the services supplied by the operating system, and develop their own versions of them, and so on.

Stopping this kind of behavior is not easy (it requires awareness building and establishment and reinforcement of specific competencies) but can quickly pay for itself in terms of reduced work effort and improved component-reuse levels.

The Self-Directed Team Myth

We saw a common approach to solving the effectiveness challenge facing the IS organization that involved the creation and dispatch of self-directed work teams. Organizations that adopted this approach often did so with almost religious zeal. Their logic went something like this:

> *We need to get closer to our customers. Our current hierarchical structure and management processes won't let us do that, so we need to change them, but that will take too long. So let's break the IS resources up into teams, let them loose to figure out for themselves how to solve the customer's problem and everything will sort itself out. We won't need to invest in methodologies or common tools or infrastructure. We will invest in the assets we already have—our* people! *All we will need is a lot of empowered teams.*

Organizations using this approach talk a lot about "empowerment" and "self-direction." They hand out a few (often excellent) required reading lists on effective teaming and set up their new team structures. They launch the "teams" approach with considerable fanfare. They adopt a "hands-off" management approach so that the teams feel free to chart their own course. Then they hit reality.

Few of the newly empowered teams seem fully to achieve the

desired results. Productivity takes a major dive. Work piles up. To see why all this happens, we need to revisit the efficiency versus effectiveness issues discussed earlier. Self-managed teams can indeed get close to their customers, and freeing them from the burdens of old organizational structures and management styles often helps here. But if self-managed teams is the only strategy, the gains in effectiveness are soon lost when it comes time to deliver. Unless the efficiency of the IS organization is improved at the same time, the customer expectations raised by the IS teams will fail to be met by the old, low-productivity development-and-delivery processes.

The "This Too Shall Pass" Myth

Although many IS organizations will admit that there is a need to improve their performance, most believe that, since they have managed to survive through the turbulent times of the 1980s and early 1990s relatively unscathed, "business as usual" will continue to work for them. They have seen the recurrent attempts to introduce new tools, work processes, or management styles. These have all come and gone, but the need for their work remains. So why worry? This will just be another passing phase, another *initiative du jour*.

This time, though, it may actually be different. Let me share with you a story told to me in early 1994 by the CIO of a very large European high-technology manufacturing business. He had been hired-in to run the IS organization 15 months earlier, with a simple brief—"Cut the number of people you have in IS in half inside 12 months."

The staffing level when he started was a little over 650 in development and maintenance, with another 150 in operations and support. Here, in essence, is how he did it.

> *When I started, I had no real idea of whether this was possible or how to go about it. Everyone seemed to be busy, so*

there was no obvious slack to cut out. Then I took a look around at what the IS staff were actually doing. I found that we had a large group of people (in the end it turned out to be about 70) who spent all their time evaluating products that we might want to use somewhere inside the IS organization. I thought this seemed excessive, but the reality was worse. In the previous two years we had spent over 250,000 hours in these evaluation exercises without selecting a single product and deploying it! We had run five so-called pilots, but none of them had resulted in a product adoption. Here was my first area to cut. Next I discovered that we had nearly 200 people working on "defect repair"—basically they were fixing problems caused by someone else in the IS organization. A lot of the people on the "repair crew" were contractors and we were paying them a lot of money to fix problems we had mostly created for ourselves. So we ran a quick defect source analysis and discovered that most of the problems were being caused by two large project teams that were staffed with poorly trained developers, a constantly changing set of outside contractors and that were appallingly badly managed. We shut them both down and shifted the critical parts of their work elsewhere. With a little tidying up in other project teams we reduced the defect rate by 90 percent within three months. I didn't need most of my repair crew any more, either. Finally, I found three projects that had been going on for more than five years without delivering anything. Each year they had "re-scoped" the project—supposedly at the "customer's" request. One of the teams was building a work management system for a division that we had sold to another company the year before. The other two had no visible customer either. So we shut them all down. By the end of the year, I had just 390 people in the IS Organization. Our delivery rate was about the same, or a little improved, but our quality was way up, so much better that our customers were beginning to notice and be complimentary about our work.

So much for business as usual. I've collected a number of similar stories over that past two years. Whether it's staff reductions, reorganizations, or outsourcing, things are changing for the IS organization in many businesses. Even, perhaps especially, in the successful ones. This time, "this too shall NOT pass."

Confusing Productivity with Cycle Time Reduction

Although the research that led to this book was primarily concerned with doing things *faster*, all the participants were also concerned with the *productivity* of the people who would work in the accelerated processes we were identifying. Because much of our initial acceleration practices were concerned with the elimination of unnecessary work (to be discussed in a later section), we were making people more productive, as well as faster. But there are limits to this productivity gain as additional acceleration strategies are applied.

Productivity vs. Speed

Our measures of productivity were based on the quantity of resource required to create an acceptable deliverable. For any given initial baseline, there will be a minimum amount of necessary work to create the finished deliverable at a defined level of quality. This will generally be an unobtainable minimum, first, because we won't usually be able to operate a perfect (right the first time) discovery process, and second, we will often have overall resource optimization and scheduling objectives for the project (or across projects) that will be suboptimal for any particular deliverable.

Provided that we take into account sources of variability in the development of the deliverables, however, we can construct a normalized productivity index and use it to calibrate the processes we use. This approach has some interesting consequences when we factor-in the desire for cycle time reduction.

When "Faster" Implies Doing More but Productivity Requires Doing Less

Joint Application Design (JAD) is a good example.[10] JAD accelerates the requirements-discovery process by bringing together representatives of all interested constituencies and using a facilitated workshop process to draw out as complete a set of requirements as possible, usually within one to two elapsed weeks. A prototype is often constructed in parallel with the workshop process so that participants are confident that their requirements have been understood and will be satisfied by the proposed solution.

Contrast this with the more conventional approach of a series of interviews with customers; written requirements specifications; executive review; requirements amendment; possible additional review/amendment iterations; and then the start of the design process.

The JAD process, when well executed, can reduce the requirements-discovery process cycle time from several months to a couple of weeks, often with an improved result. It does, however, require a significant resource commitment from a skilled and generally busy group of people. Traditional methods require only a small number of analysts, limited logistics support, and limited project management. JAD requires specialist facilitators and subject matter experts. There must be extensive logistics support and participative project management. Technology infrastructure may be required and must be supported.

In total, the JAD process can consume up to twice the resources required for the conventional approach. It also requires specialist roles, such as the facilitator. The staff who fill these roles may not be used much between JAD sessions, and will hence seem

[10] *Joint Application Design*, by Judy H. August. Englewood Cliffs, NJ: Yourdon Press/Prentice-Hall, 1991.

to have low productivity. The price is worth paying because we get a good result five to ten times faster, but there is a price nonetheless. Simply looking at productivity issues will make the cycle time compression look unattractive. Instead, we should focus on cycle time reduction, and the consequent early delivery of business benefits, as the primary objective, but recognize that the processes used to meet this objective should be as efficient and productive as possible.

Part II

Redefining the IS Organization

5

The IT Process Landscape

Taking a Process View of the Management of Information Technology

Fueled by dramatic demands for business change, leading companies are turning to process management to achieve both incremental and radical performance improvement.[1] Judging from conversations with clients and others, we think it is fair to say we are in the midst of a process revolution. Process management offers a way for organizations to reduce cost, improve quality, and cut cycle time in virtually everything that they do. These same benefits are available to Information Systems (IS) organizations that choose to institute the process management concept.

Tom Davenport has identified three principal benefits of adopting a process perspective on information technology (IT) processes.[2] First, a process perspective is essentially synonymous with a customer perspective. Since, by definition, a process must have a customer, process thinking forces an organization to focus on its customers. Second, process thinking encourages process management. With that kind of quantification comes a clearer vision of what an organization should be trying to achieve, and allows it to focus on how to do it. This point is particularly relevant for IS professionals, many of whom view their work as a "craft" as opposed to a predictable, repeatable process.

The first step in process management is to define the overall set of processes (and their interrelationships) that constitute the *process landscape*. Further process understanding involves determining current process flows and collecting baseline perfor-

[1]This chapter is based on a series of working papers developed as part of the Ernst & Young Total Quality Management for Information Services (TQM-IS) Leadership program during 1992 and 1993. This material was originally developed by Mary Silva Doctor and Charlie Gold of the E&Y LLP Center for Business Innovation in Boston.

[2]"What Is an IS Process?," by Thomas H. Davenport. TQM-IS Research Note, January 1992.

mance data about current processes. This process-definition information can then serve as the foundation for improvement or innovation activities.

This chapter defines a generic landscape of information technology processes. We define IT processes as those business processes that are associated with the creation and ongoing management of an enterprise's IT resources. As we will discuss later in this chapter, these IT processes are actually just one element of an enterprise's overall business process landscape. This definition of IT process is *independent of functional boundaries*, since IT creation and management activities occur throughout an organization, not just in an IS function or organization.[3] However, as the IS function is *primarily responsible* for these activities in most organizations at the present time, the set of generic IT processes we have defined also largely encompasses those processes associated with managing the IS function or organizational units. In many respects, therefore, the IT process landscape described in this chapter is defined from the perspective of the IS organization.

These generic IT process definitions can be used in at least three ways. First, as mentioned above, it is important to understand the IT process landscape in order to understand the *extent* of IT processes. This knowledge is important in IT strategy and planning activities as well as in determining the appropriate process structure against which to apply total quality management (TQM) improvement principles. Second, the generic process set can be a resource that organizations use as a template during development of their own IT process definitions and implementation of process-management activities. Finally, we used this IT process landscape as a common framework for managing the research activities within the various research programs whose results are reported in this book.

The IT process definitions presented here were developed through analysis of the existing IT process definitions at some of

[3]Hence the use of "IT" processes, and not just "IS" processes, which would limit us to the work of the IS organization or function.

the companies participating in the research program, as well as through discussions with individuals from these same organizations and others.

Like so many activities, process definition and management are continuous learning exercises. Process definitions cannot and should not be cast in concrete. Process boundaries need to be assigned based on business requirements and capabilities and should be modified as these change. Therefore, this material must be viewed as an iteration in a learning process as opposed to the absolute and final truth. To illustrate this point, at least one company, whose processes we studied, redefined their set of IT processes during the time we were conducting our research.

What Is a Business Process?

Business processes are a set of logically related tasks performed to achieve a defined business outcome. Processes have two important characteristics.

First, processes have customers. In other words, there is a recipient for the outcome of the process. While identifying IT-process customers, it became clear that a process often serves more than one customer set. Often there is one type of customer that funds or sponsors an initiative but never actually uses the end product. For example, an executive might sponsor the acquisition of a new payroll system but will never actually use the system himself. We identified this type of customer as the primary customer. All other customer segments were identified as secondary customers. In the payroll system example above, a secondary customer would be the accounting clerk who uses the system daily. It is important to recognize the different customer segments, because each will have different requirements and expectations from IT-process activities. A customer may be internal or external to the organization.

Second, process structures are independent of an organization's functional boundaries. Given this definition, examples of processes include developing new products, ordering goods from

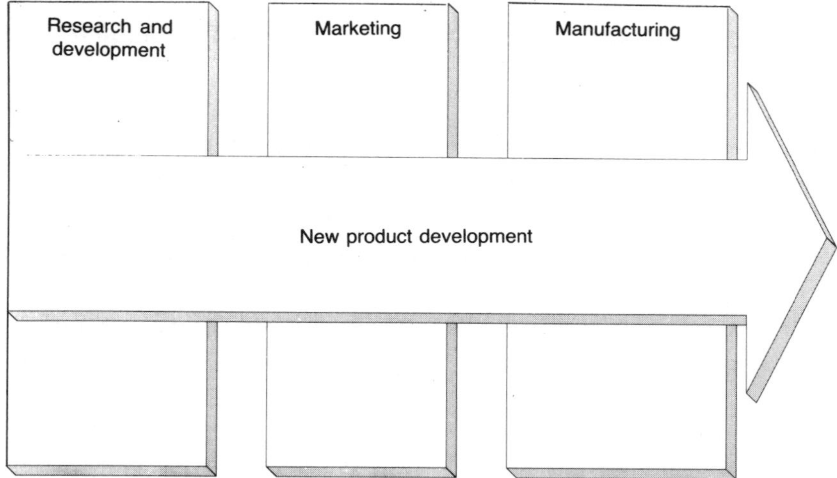

Figure 5.1 *New product development as an example of a process that crosses functional boundaries.*

suppliers, and developing a marketing plan. As Figure 5.1 illustrates, a new product-development process encompasses activities in the research and development, marketing, and manufacturing functions.

A business process essentially defines how work is structured at a relatively high level of abstraction. A company need not, and should not, view a business process as bounded by its existing or future organizational boundaries. While most organizations begin their focus on business processes that lie within their enterprise boundaries, a business process may equally be viewed as cross-enterprise as well. Some well-known examples of process-innovation involved process activities that span more than one company.[4] With options such as the outsourcing of various IT activities, organi-

[4]Lithonia Lighting, a leading lighting manufacturer, is an example of an organization that looked beyond its own boundaries as a way to maintain its market-leading position. Using information technology, Lithonia linked the various contractors, distributors, and agents who must work together to service customers.

zations may find that IT processes can cross enterprise boundaries as well.

A business process virtually always contains several lower-level processes, which we call *sub-processes*. These sub-processes define the structure of work at a more detailed, but still fairly abstract, level. The sub-process structure is a hierarchy. Therefore, sub-processes may also contain additional sub-processes. For example, within the IT process of "IT Component Delivery and Evolution," which we will describe later, we typically find sub-processes such as business-requirements analysis, application development, systems testing, and system installation or deployment.

What is the "right" number of processes for such a generic set? There currently is no hard and fast rule with respect to this question. Indeed, there is no definite number of processes even within one organization. Rather, how they are defined depends on the purpose at hand. Individual companies that have defined and articulated their IT processes have commonly enumerated between five and ten. When determining the number of IT processes it will have, an organization must trade-off between having a greater potential for process-innovation benefits and having a manageable project scope. With fewer processes, an organization will have a greater possibility of innovation through process integration. However, having fewer processes, each with a larger scope, also presents greater challenges in understanding, measuring, and changing each process.

When defining IT processes, companies need to view definition and boundary-setting primarily as a scope issue. Each process must be small enough to be understandable. When process definitions are more focused, change management is only very difficult, rather than impossible.

We have encountered a common barrier when working with companies to define processes. Process management demands a different view of an organization and, if implemented, can lead to dramatic organizational change. Thus, executives sometimes confuse process definition with organizational design. We have seen many instances where process definitions align with the existing organization structure. To the extent that these can be viewed separately, it will be less challenging to define meaningful processes for the purposes of improvement and innovation. Any organizational redesign is best if it *follows* from the understanding that is developed through process management. Also, organizations need to recognize that if process boundaries are narrowed and, thus, do not cross existing organizational and functional boundaries, they probably will not realize the levels of expected performance improvement.

The IT Processes

We have divided the spectrum of IT activities into seven IT processes:

1. IT-Enabled Business Opportunity Identification
2. IT Infrastructure Stewardship
3. IT Component Delivery and Evolution
4. IT Operations
5. IT Customer Support
6. IT Strategy Development
7. IS Management

Figure 5.2 depicts the overall relationship of these seven IT processes. As we mentioned previously, we defined the generic landscape of IT processes presented here after studying the IT processes of five companies that participated in our research. These companies represented a variety of industries and were of different sizes. Interestingly, there was a high degree of similarity in their selection of process boundaries and definitions. However, some of the landscape's generic processes were not found in any company's current process set. These processes emerged following discussions with individuals from these companies and others about emerging IT and business trends and strategies. In this way, the landscape of IT processes is being used to emphasize certain activities. Some

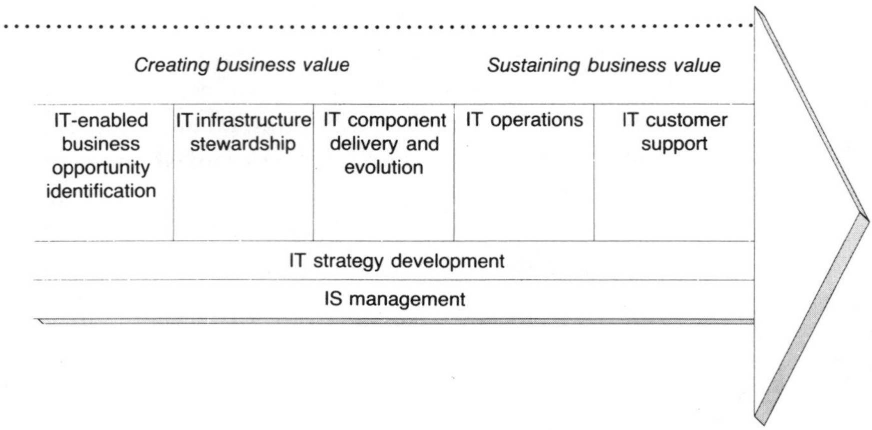

Creating business value | *Sustaining business value*

IT-enabled business opportunity identification	IT infrastructure stewardship	IT component delivery and evolution	IT operations	IT customer support
IT strategy development				
IS management				

Figure 5.2 *The IT process landscape.*

of these activities are ones where a company must focus its attention if IT is to be fully exploited. Others are areas where IS can and should play a more prominent role.

The test of each process was that it deliver important products and/or services to the enterprise. The passage of this test is easily seen for five of the processes, which can be viewed as the IT "production" processes. These processes, which are depicted in the diagram as a "value chain," deliver value to the enterprise. The first three (IT-Enabled Business Opportunity Identification, IT Infrastructure Stewardship, and IT Component Delivery and Evolution) are involved with creating future value for the organization. While developing a new application system does not provide immediate value to the enterprise, the product will do so someday. Therefore, these processes need to be viewed as *investment* activities. The last two production processes (IT Operations and IT Customer Support) are associated with delivering present value by *providing ongoing IT services and capabilities* to the organization.

The two remaining processes—we call these the "support" processes—are IT Strategy Development and IS Management. They grew out of a recognition that certain activities are required to set the stage for, and then manage the production processes. Though the products and/or services of these support processes are less tangible than those of the production processes, they are still very real and important. For example, IS Management *includes tactical project management* and *oversight planning* activities that underlie and touch on each of the five production processes. IT Strategy Development applies to a broader, enterprise-wide view of IT.

IS Management is more inwardly focused, referring to the business management of the IS function/organization. We have therefore made the distinction in naming the process *IS* Management, rather than *IT* Management.

Each of these seven processes is described in the following sections in terms of its purpose, the products and/or services that the process delivers to the organization, customers of the process, and some key sub-processes making up the process. A consolidated list of IT processes and sub-processes is provided in Appendix 4.

IT-Enabled Business Opportunity Identification

Information technology is recognized as one of a handful of enablers, including organizational and human factors, to major organizational change.[5] IT can be used to restructure processes in a number of ways, including automation or improved information access.

The purpose of this process is to ensure strategic business change activities fully exploit IT-enabled opportunities. This process is instrumental in creating future business value from IT investments. This objective is accomplished through increasing the organization's awareness of the potential benefits and opportunities offered by IT. Increased awareness is created through an assort-

[5]See *Process Innovation: Reengineering Work through Information Technology*, by Thomas Davenport. Boston: Harvard Business School Press, 1992, for a taxonomy of the ways in which information technology can proide the tools to restructure business processes.

ment of seemingly unrelated activities. A successful IT-Enabled Business Opportunity Identification process enables an organization to capitalize on the business advantages of IT. The products and services include proposals for business process innovation, assessments of the applicability of emerging technologies, and executive education. Senior business executives are the primary customers of this process.

One factor that caused us to delineate this process was the increasingly prominent role that IT plays in business process change activities. A majority of the participants in our research programs viewed improvement and innovation of business processes as a strategic business thrust that must involve the IS organization. Explicit acknowledgment of these activities is the first step toward ensuring such a focus.

Many different sub-processes lie within the IT-Enabled Business Opportunity Identification process. These sub-processes tend to emphasize business-process change activities. The significant IT-related sub-processes include: participation and/or leadership in business-process innovation; education and development of enterprise decision-makers fully to utilize IT resources; exploration and evaluation of emerging information technologies; enhancement of existing IT capability usage; and involvement of IS in the business strategy and planning activities of the enterprise.

Based on examination of the sub-processes, it is clear that the IT-enabled Business Opportunity Identification process spans IS and other business functions. Thus, leadership for and involvement in its various sub-processes may come from a variety of sources. Armed with their IT and systems approach knowledge, IS professionals need to play a key, and sometimes leadership, role in its execution.

IT Infrastructure Stewardship

The purpose of this process is to define and design the IT infrastructure for the enterprise. It should be noted that this process addresses infrastructure *design* exclusively. Infrastructure component development/acquisition and implementation are subsumed within IT Component Delivery and Evolution. An IT infrastructure is defined as hardware, software, and information elements that are a shareable, enterprise-wide resource.[6] While business units and functions might understand what technology and information are needed to run their businesses, there needs to be a global, enterprise-wide perspective on the use of IT as well. This perspective is essential to assure integration, provide flexibility, and minimize redundancies and costs. The purpose of this process is to maintain this view while creating the flexible, rapid response environment so necessary for the success of business units in today's competitive marketplace.

Establishing and maintaining an infrastructure is a challenge facing virtually all companies. Discussions of infrastructure are becoming increasingly common in the IT management literature. IS executives view infrastructure as one of their most critical areas of interest.[7] Promoting IT infrastructure within an organization is a particularly daunting challenge because infrastructure elements are not as visible to end users and executives as specific applications. In addition, infrastructure investments are virtually impossible to justify using traditional methods, such as Return on Investment or Internal Rate of Return, because they have less direct impact on business results.

One reason for explicitly defining this IT process is to promote infrastructure thinking. Some organizations have been successful in this endeavor. One technology manufacturer, for example, has established an IT evaluation process that assesses the technology and infrastructure implications of a proposed project independently and on a par with analysis of the financial and strategic returns.

Others are also realizing that there are enormous costs associ-

[6]"The Role and Value of Information Technology Infrastructure: Some Empirical Observations," by Peter Weill. CISR working paper No. 240, May 1992.

[7]Information Management Issues for the 1990s, by Fred Niederman, James Branchau, and James C. Weatherbe. *MIS Quarterly*, December 1991, p. 481.

ated with not taking an infrastructure view. One financial services firm that we worked with elected not to establish any enterprise-wide standard for electronic mail. As a result, each business unit purchased its own e-mail system. Over time, the company acquired 14 different systems. During a benchmarking exercise with a competitor, the company discovered that this decision put them at a multi-million dollar cost disadvantage annually.

The primary customers of the IT Infrastructure Stewardship process are the key senior executives responsible for the health and future of the enterprise. The secondary customers include all the employees who will work within the architectures and structures of the enterprise's IT infrastructure. The process products include IT architecture definitions, enterprise models, and architectural policies and standards. Sub-processes include defining the IT architecture, developing and maintaining enterprise models, assisting units in the use of the infrastructure, and establishing the knowledge base/repository.

IT Component Delivery and Evolution

This purpose of this process is to acquire, develop, and deliver new hardware, software, and information components for the enterprise. Included in this process is the adaptation and/or evolution of existing components, as needed, to meet changing business requirements. Like the two preceding processes, this process is focused on the creation of future business value. IT Component Delivery and Evolution encompasses the development and deployment of both *business solutions* and *infrastructure components* for the enterprise.

The primary products and services are new and/or improved hardware, software, and information components. Although all IT users will use the products of this process, the primary customers are business managers who sponsor these activities.

There are a number of sub-processes within this process including: defining component projects, analyzing business requirements, producing conceptual system design, investigating component purchase, producing technical design, purchasing/building elements of component, and delivery or deployment of component. Selecting the appropriate sub-processes to use in a given situation will depend on the desired end product (e.g., application software, hardware). Thus, for all IT Component Delivery and Evolution process initiatives, there needs to be an initial, common activity of selecting the correct sub-processes for a particular project. This is an important activity, which is one aspect of the sub-process, Defining Component Project. An objective of this key sub-process is to ensure the requirements of the project are addressed by the appropriate sub-processes in light of the desired end-product, as well as the IT strategy and infrastructure principles and policies of the enterprise.

Though the overall IT Component Delivery and Evolution process has a strong *product* orientation, the accompanying service elements (e.g., training, systems deployment, organizational change management, project management) must not be overlooked. It is not enough to say a defect-free product is the goal of this process. Rather, satisfaction of the enterprise's business needs through delivery of an appropriate "IT solution" that is well utilized effectively by its intended customers, must be the objective.

IT Operations

In moving from the IT Component Delivery and Evolution Process to IT Operations, we also cross the boundary from processes focused on *creating future value* to those aimed at providing or giving support to installed products and components. These are *sustaining processes*. Once a new system or infrastructure component is deployed, it must be accessible to those business users that need it. The purpose of this process is to support the ongoing operational requirements of the enterprise. This process contains the activities that provide access to the enterprise's IT resources. The products and services of the process include access to application systems, to information warehouses or databases, and to computing resources.

This process may have a very broad customer base. The customers are all users of the enterprise's IT capabilities. As an example of the pervasiveness of IT in today's businesses and the extent of the customer base, one telecommunications company told us that over 97 percent of their employees use IT in performing their jobs. In some organizations that provide external suppliers and customers with direct access to information systems, the process boundaries extend well beyond those of the organization itself.

One sub-process is the provision of the operational IT environment, which encompasses the traditional "glass house" data center, as well as the desktop. Additional sub-processes include activities associated with scheduling and tracking the usage of resources, controlling and managing the IT environment to ensure integrity and security, and monitoring performance.

IT Customer Support

Once IT systems are operational, there needs to be a mechanism for their users to ask questions and report problems, and for these questions or problems to be resolved. The purpose of this process is to provide that service to the customers of IT. There is also a proactive dimension of this process, which is involved with preventing problems in the IT environment as well as training new users of the enterprise IT capabilities. Fielding operational questions, resolving problems, problem prevention, assistance in negotiating the IT environment, are all products and services of this process. The scope of this process encompasses IT regardless of its location, whether it is in a central facility or a desktop workstation.

Fielding and answering customer questions about operations, often through a "help desk," is a common example of the type of activity in this process. An analogy from a broader business perspective would be toll-free numbers (e.g., "800" numbers), that many corporations have set up to field inquiries. These numbers are most useful when the corporation has a broad customer base. It is less confusing and frustrating for customers to call a single number regardless of the question, rather than remember whom to call when a particular problem arises. For this reason, some IS organizations are considering establishing "vertical" help desks so IT customers can call one number no matter what the question.

Another key sub-process within the customer-support process is assisting customers in navigating the enterprise's IT environment. A challenging and major cause of lost productivity for information workers is locating the information they need to do their jobs in an enterprise's assorted databases. One service of this sub-process is providing ad hoc assistance to these information workers in locating and providing information. In an enterprise with a function-rich infrastructure, customer support could also assist users in finding the function they need as well. The remaining two proceses, the IT support processes, are described next.

IT Strategy Development

The purpose of this process is to establish a long-term direction for the IT resources of the enterprise that will enable the organization to meet its business goals while optimizing its existing and future investments in IT. The primary products are documents such as mission statements, visions, organization designs, and road maps for developing and improving IT resources. While IS professionals are the actual users of the IT strategy products, such as the planning documents, the primary customers are key business stakeholders. Stakeholders are the primary customers because the products are an integral part of overall enterprise management.

Strategy documents become increasingly important as more organizations distribute decision-making authority and empower employees. As more organizations empower employees and disperse decision-making responsibility more widely, mission statements and goals are vital elements providing employees with the information they need to make appropriate decisions. Strategy documents provide the framework in which each individual or project team should operate to contribute to the enterprise's overall goals and directions.

Sub-processes within IT Strategy Development include determining the strategy, pacing, and priorities of key strategic initiatives, establishing the guiding IT principles/standards, managing IT costs/benefits, determining the optimal IT organization design, and establishing IT human resource policies.

IS Management

This process is devoted to managing the IS "business." The products and services include budgets, performance appraisals, training plans, equipment allocation plans, status reports, improvement plans, and IS performance measurements. The primary customers are key stakeholders. Secondary customers are IS professionals who benefit from the products of this process.

Sub-processes include hiring, promoting, developing, and retraining IS employees and financial and budgeting activities. Two key sub-processes in this area are measuring and monitoring IS performance, and IT improvement. The purpose of the measurement sub-process is to establish measures that IS managers can use in assessing the performance of the IS function as well as important IS activities, such as strategic projects.[8] The second key process, coordination of IT improvement, is closely aligned with measurement and performance management. This sub-process would include any activities aimed at improving IT processes. For example, Development Center activities would be included in this sub-process.

Relationship of the IT Process Landscape to Overall Business Processes

IT processes are a subset of an organization's overall business processes. At the enterprise level, most organizations define one or two business processes associated with the management of IT.

[8] For more information on measurement, see "IS Measures—A Balancing Act," research note by Charles Gold, available from the Ernst & Young Center for Business Innovation, One Walnut Street, Boston, MA 02108.

While certain IT processes are, in fact, sub-processes of these business processes, others are sub-processes within business change processes. For example, the IT-Enabled Business Opportunity Identification might be part of the overall business planning and development processes through its contribution to the consideration of the strategic implications of IT. Even IT Component Delivery and Evolution can be viewed as a sub-process in a product-development process, if the new product or processes spawned by the product require new information systems.

An area of growing interest in American business, that will influence this relationship, is the management of information *per se*, regardless of the storage medium (e.g., electronic, paper) or form (e.g., document, data item). Management theorists have, for some time, talked of effective information management as a key to success in the current world economy.[9] Modern business enterprises are essentially information-processing entities. Out of this thinking has grown a desire to better understand information management. While information-management thinking is still in its infancy, it is clear that IT processes are a subset of a broader set of information-management processes. IT processes address information that is captured, stored, and distributed using information technology. As the principles of information management are further developed, the IT processes will undoubtedly evolve.

The definition of IT processes offers a foundation for improving the management and development of new capabilities of an enterprise's IT resource and the way that IT-related services are provided to the organization. While the IS organization is the primary locus for most of these processes in today's environment, one trend appears to be an increase in the migration of responsibility for IT processes into other organization units. Thus it is increasingly important to identify explicitly an organization's IT processes so that they are not overlooked as business-improvement prospects. The IT processes described above provide a starting point for this

[9] See, for example, The Coming of the New Organization, by Peter F. Drucker. *Harvard Business Review*, January–February 1988, p. 45.

necessary management activity. However, as we noted at the start of this chapter, they are but a stage along the continuous journey of learning.

The Process Footprint

Now that we have established a generic process view of the activities associated with the management of IT in an organization, we can look at each of the processes, in turn, to see how well each operates, both in relation to other processes within the landscape, and to best practices. What we will discover, in general, is that any particular enterprise has a variety of process states. Some processes will be recently improved or innovated; others will not have changed for many years. Some processes will be examples of or close to, best practices. Others will lag very far from best practice, even so far as to be dysfunctional ("broken"), or unnecessary.

In this way, we can construct a "footprint" that categorizes where an enterprise or its IS organization stands with respect to the process of the IT landscape. This will give us an initial high-level "map" of where we should focus for maximum impact when seeking improvement or innovation opportunities. Although we have developed our own footprint model from our multi-client research, others have followed similar lines of thinking, generally coming to very similar conclusions.[10]

Characteristics of Process

In defining the process footprint, we first identify the characteristics of the various IT processes that are important to the effective use of the process. In order to keep the model simple and manageable, we look at only six characteristics:

[10] Spinning a Footprint of Business, IT Readiness, by Howard Rubin. *Application Development Trends*, Vol. 1, No. 11, pp. 27–32.

1. **The "age" of the process.** When was the process first introduced or last changed in a significant way?
2. **The "coverage" of the process.** How many of those who should use the process actually do so on a regular basis?
3. **The "coherence" of the process.** How consistent is the use of the process from person (or team) to person, and from time to time?
4. **The "quality" of the process.** What is the density of defects that can be attributed to the process?
5. **The "value" of the process.** How much of the process contributes to a value-added output?
6. **The "benchmark" for the process.** How does the process compare with the best-known practice?

Each of these six characteristics is assessed on a scale from 1 to 5. From these six characteristics, we can construct a "radar plot" of the scores that define the footprint. An example is given in Figure 5.3.

Process Maturity Profiles

In an evolving organization, processes are not static. When a process is first introduced, it will need adjustment to match the specific demands of its customesr, just as software does. As improvements are made, the process matures and, over time, becomes a better match to the business objectives it serves. These objectives will also change, however, so the improvement process must be continuous. At some stage the original process design, although capable of further improvement, no longer returns sufficient benefits to justify continuing to improve it. At this point a new process must be developed, usually through innovation, and implemented, starting the life cycle over again. At any point in time, therefore, the IT process landscape and its footprint can be assessed for overall and individual maturity (see Figure 5.4).

Processes within the landscape will tend to mature at different rates. Rates of maturity depend as much on the characteristics of

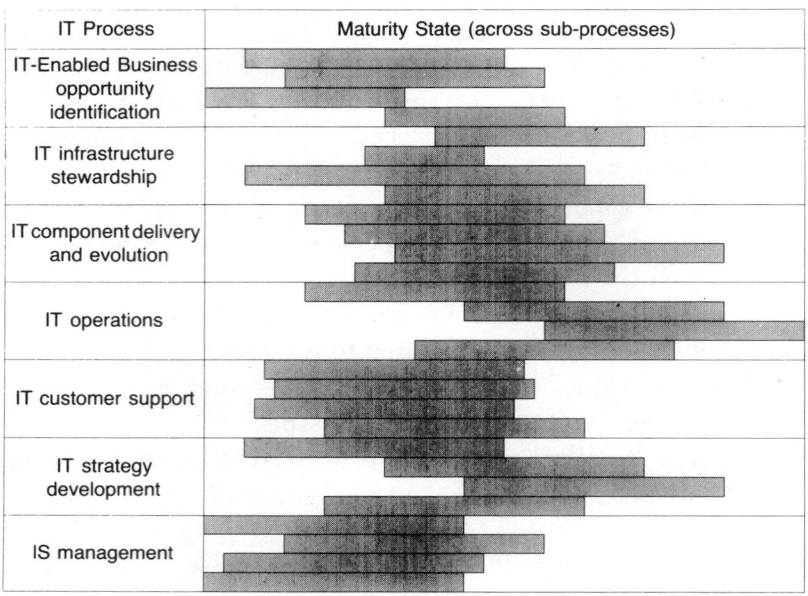

Figure 5.3 *Example of a process footprint.*

the process as on the IS organization's willingness to improve or innovate its processes. Thus planning processes often change rapidly. Administration processes do not. It can be argued that all of an organization's processes should be at about the same level of maturity, so that they function together smoothly, and the different maturity profiles will ensure that the organization does not have to innovate all of its process at once when improvement opportunities are exhausted.[11] In practice, we have yet to see an organization in which all the IT processes were at the same level of maturity. This has an interesting consequence for the required style of effective process management.

[11] See, for instance, Process Management Adapts Application Development to Users, by John R. Vacca. *Application Development Trends*, Vol. 1, No. 3, pp. 47–55.

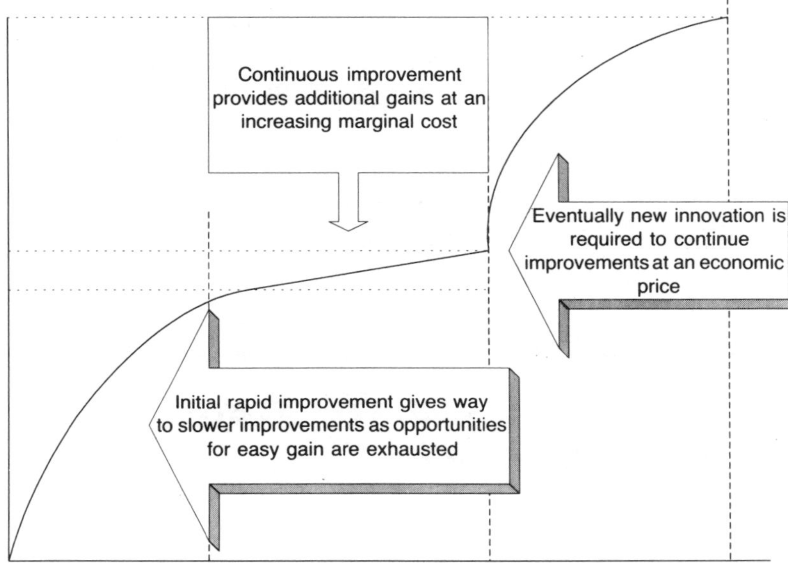

Figure 5.4 *Example of a process-maturity life cycle.*

Management Styles for Processes with Different Characteristics

Remember the three approaches to coordination and control for a process that we introduced back in the section on management myths in Chapter 4? These approaches translate very nicely into three styles of process management.

1. When a process is new and still being implemented, a mutual-adjustment style of management works very well.
2. As a process matures, and improvements lead to wider adoption and successful use, the supervision style becomes more appropriate.

3. As the process becomes more difficult to improve, and nears the end of its useful life, the most appropriate style makes transitions toward standardization.

Over the life cycle of a process we will need all three types at some time—matching the appropriate approach to the level of process maturity. As the process matures, so must the management style.

What Parts of the Process Landscape Do We Want to Accelerate?

Thoughts on Targeting Processes for Innovation or Improvement

Once IT processes are defined and a process footprint is created, what comes next? The next logical step is to begin to improve them. This will initially involve determining current process flows and collecting baseline performance data. As we discussed earlier, a company needs to choose the magnitude of improvement desired, since that dictates which improvement approach to use—continuous improvement or process innovation. If a company elects to institute a continuous improvement approach, the sub-processes become the appropriate level of focus. The overall process is the appropriate scope when innovation is the goal.

An IS organization does not need to choose between process innovation or continuous improvement. It can be doing both at the same time for different target processes. For example, a company might decide that innovation is in order for the IT Component Delivery and Evolution process, while continuous improvement is more appropriate for IT Operations. Such choices are to be expected. Indeed, it would be beyond the resources of almost any organization to innovate all IT processes at the same time.

Given scarce resources, an organization must prioritize among processes and target those linked to the issues at hand. One further consideration is organizational readiness for change. An aspect of this regard is the maturity and state of the current process. For instance, some organizations are using the Software Engineering Institute's Capability Maturity Model to assess the current state of the software development sub-process, which is a part of IT Component Delivery and Evolution, and to identify improvement actions.[12] The capability Maturity Model, for example, helps management understand where the software-development process stands and the readiness of the organization to embark on the next improvement step. There are different ways to select a process for innovation. One way might be to choose the IT process(es) most central to achieving the organization's goals. For example, an organization could map its IT processes to business goals to see which will have the most strategic impact. This analysis would reveal which processes are important from a strategic perspective. In this case, innovation of these strategic processes would provide the most value to the enterprise.

Another way to choose a target process is to select the IT process which affects the greatest number of people within the enterprise. This might be one way to maximize the immediate value delivered by the innovation activities. With everyone within the business who uses IT as a customer base, IT Operations and IT Customer Support are the most pervasive IT processes. However, it is important to note that, while innovating these processes might improve overall customer satisfaction, these might not be the "right" ones to innovate from a strategic perspective.

Economics of Software Ownership

In practice, most of the costs of software occur *after* the development process is complete, not during the development process. Lifetime costs associated with continuing enhancement and fault-

[12]"Capability Maturity Model for Software," by Mark C. Paulk et al. Software Engineering Institute, August 1991.

fixing will usually outweigh the initial development costs by a factor of ten or more. We should therefore look at the economics of software as being determined by the "Create, Operate/Modify/ Improve, Retire" sequence rather than just the "Create" element, as we have traditionally done. After all, successful software will be in use for up to 25 or more years, even though it may have been modified or enhanced many times during its life-in-use.

Taking a Whole-Life-Cycle View of Software Costs

If we look at the costs of software over an entire life-in-use cycle, we get a different economic picture for the development-and-delivery process. Firstly, we will see that the majority of costs accrue after implementation, as we modify or improve the application. Since these change processes are inevitable (the software must change to meet changing business needs), we should plan to make them as easy as possible in the initial development. Second, we will discover the need for a set of disposability strategies—planning in advance for the complete retirement of some or all of our applications. It is amazing how difficult it is to completely retire a suite of software. We consistently found applications that were more than 20 years old and collected many stories of applications that were only retired when the hardware products that they ran on finally become unavailable.

Design for Maintainability Issues

Design for maintainability adds cost to the development process. Building-in an awareness of such factors as design and code understandability and testability requires time and effort that would not otherwise be invested in the application. Creating an application design and an architecture for application integration that is robust and resilient to changes in the application components requires a higher level of skill than do more straightforward development approaches. This also adds to the cost of the development phase.

The bottom line in all of this: *does the design for maintainability approach save more than it costs and, if so, how much more?* This is an area where we have too little data (because too few organizations have a design for maintainability process that has operated for long enough to generate meaningful comparisons). Comparative experience in other "manufacturing" processes is useful but not easily transferable to software development, for reasons that we have already seen.

Our best guess is that effective design for maintainability has an initial heavy "engineering" cost, but that this reduces as the development process is redesigned to accommodate the maintainability objective. Overall, design for maintainability probably increases development costs by about 50 percent. In return, we can probably reduce the effort to maintain by about half. Since the effort to maintain (based on historic data) is about ten times the cost to develop, this is a very worthwhile investment, but we must once more beware the short-term productivity pursuit that might make our revised development process look unattractive.

Design for Usability Issues

One final thought in this part of our search for accelerated software development. In his excellent book *The Design of Everyday Things*, Donald Norman points out that much of what we build is poorly designed for its purpose.[13] As a result, we expend a great deal of effort to overcome the shortcomings of the tools we use. The same can be said of the majority of business software. The concepts of "performance-centered design"—building applications that enhance their users' ability to perform the work that the application supports—is still relatively new and little practiced. Yet it has the potential to deliver significant value to a business that can master the approach.

[13] *The Design of Everyday Things*, by Donald A. Norman. New York: Basic Books, 1988.

Performance-centered design also costs more, requires more skilled application designers, and demands a more complex development-and-testing process. We don't really know how much more expensive it might be. How much might it save? We don't really know that either, but the potential from early attempts seems very large.

PART III

Acceleration Strategies for Information Systems Delivery

6

Taxonomy of Acceleration Strategies

To help with cataloging the available acceleration strategies that our research uncovered, we first developed a simple, five-part taxonomy for organizing the objectives of a performance-improvement program aimed at cycle time reduction. Acceleration strategies could then be assigned to one or more of these groups. Four of the groups of approaches were initially obvious to us from previous work in process improvement, related to the IT Process Landscape. The fifth group (*listed first* in what follows) we discovered empirically.[1] The five strategic groups of approaches are as follows:

1. **Don't try to be good at everything.** This is the management of demand.
2. **Don't do what you don't have to.** Eliminate unnecessary work from the development process for a project.
3. **Don't do anything more often than you have to.** Minimize unnecessary rework within a development project and between projects.
4. **Do as much as you can at once.** Look for opportunities for increased parallel activity.
5. **Supply and use the right processes and tools.** Find the places where tools make a difference; supply really good ones; and then give incentive to use them.

In this chapter we provide a brief summary of each of these five strategic approaches and the tools and techniques available to us if we choose to implement them.

[1]We describe the sudden discovery of an obvious phenomenon, or the attainment of an insight that, in retrospect, we should have figured out in advance as a "Blinding Flash of the Obvious" (BFO). We had quite a few BFOs during the research.

"Don't Try to Be Good at Everything": The Management of Demand

Most IS organizations build applications because someone asks them to do so. Often the customer also wants the application built in a particular way, or wants to use a specific technology or combination of technologies. If this situation is allowed to grow over time, the IS organization can be forced to develop in and support many different technology combinations.

Our research encountered this situation many times—indeed we came to think that this is a universal phenomenon unless the IS Organization has already recognized the problem and started to address it. In one fairly extreme case, the commercial banking division of a super-regional bank, we counted more than 50 different technology combinations being supported by the development and maintenance staff of a medium-sized IS shop (about 200 people). Even in very large IS groups, a similar problem exists. At a regional telephone company, we found over 170 different technology combinations being supported by about 3,000 people. In large groups the situation is complicated by divisional structures and internal organizational boundaries. As a result, some technology combinations had plenty of support. Others had hardly any. In most cases we looked at, at least four or five new technologies were being added every year (in one instance we counted over 40 introductions in a single year), but nothing ever seemed to go away unless it was an abysmal public failure on first use (and not always then). Almost everywhere we looked we saw IS organizations and individuals struggling to cope effectively with the resulting new demands for skills, knowledge, and experience.

The Minimum-Size Dilemma

It seemed fairly obvious, in hindsight, that there must be a minimum size to the resource pool needed to sustain a set of technological support capabilities in this way. We spent some time building and trying out models of the range of skills required to be really good at developing in and then supporting a modern, complex technology combination. We then tried to factor-in the effects of learning curves, competency reinforcement (you can never be good at some things if you don't do them all the time), staff turnover, and availability demands. We also tried to judge the impact of constantly shifting technology capability, even within an otherwise standard set of products. The objective was to come up with a minimum Full-Time Equivalent (FTE) figure with which we felt comfortable.

We didn't get a really convincing answer (the situational variables are too complex and there were too little comparable data with which to validate the model), but we consistently came up with a number in excess of 20 FTEs. We also discovered that there is relatively little opportunity for cross-specialization, even within the same basic areas of knowledge. Knowing how to design an *Oracle* database to get the best performance does not give you the knowledge required to do the same job for *Sybase* or *DB2*. The basics are certainly the same, but the basics aren't enough any more. And the advanced knowledge is extremely technology- or product-specific.

This is a real dilemma for small to medium IS groups faced with many technologies to support. In the example of the bank that we introduced at the beginning of this section, 200 or so people can be highly effective in supporting only 15 to 20 technology combinations at most—only about a third of the number that they were required to work with. This ratio is only achievable if the technologies are chosen for the maximum synergy in required competency (this is seldom the case), and if the resource pool is stable. In the case of the bank, neither factor was true and the number of technologies was growing every year, while the number of people was required to shrink.

Demand management attacks this problem by selecting a relatively small number of technology combinations to develop competencies around and then working with customers to make these the technologies-of-choice for all future development work. New technologies can be added, but only if some existing technology is retired at a comparable rate.

When we discussed this approach with a number of IS managers, virtually all told us that demand management would not work. If they didn't agree to do whatever their customers asked, the customers would go elsewhere and they would have even less say over the technologies chosen. They would also probably still end up being required to support the results.

"Don't Do What You Don't Have To": Elimination of Work from the Development Process for a Project

IS development-and-delivery processes are complex. Developing high-quality business software requires many different types of activity, with complex interconnections and dependencies. It is a characteristic of the processes we use that mistakes made early on tend to propagate and multiply in seriousness and consequence if they are not identified close to the point where they were first introduced. As a result, IS developers and their managers have evolved detailed work descriptions and control processes designed to detect or eliminate errors. Unfortunately, most of these controls don't work very well and all of them impose a significant resource burden on the project.

If we had a better understanding of the work that we needed to do, and a more effective set of control processes, we could design projects that are much less resource-intensive, but just as effective. This approach to *process specialization* is difficult to do without help from a sophisticated technology infrastructure, but, as we saw in Chapter 4, it can have a significant effect.

Categories of Work

Process specialization requires that we understand the many different types of work that make up an IS development project. Any taxonomy for the types of work can be debated, but we might, as an example, identify such work types as:

- The intelligent use of past experience to determine an initial project baseline;
- Investigation and discovery;
- Problem analysis and the modeling of requirements;
- Solution identification and selection;
- Transformation of requirements models to solution designs;
- Deliverable creation and installation;
- Communication;
- Implementation;
- Process management;

and so on.

Within each work type, we can define optimum working practices, which may be interdependent, or use preferred approaches to actually carrying out the work. The more specialized we choose to get, the more complex the project design process becomes and there are clear areas of diminishing returns where further specialization does not improve performance and may degrade our ability to manage the process. In general, however, we can use specialization to consistently improve our project designs over those that result from unspecialized approaches.

Speeding-Up Discovery

Discovery is the most intractable of the work types to improve. How do you ensure that you find what you are looking for when you don't know in advance what it is you are looking for, or what you will find? One of the best approaches to speeding-up discovery is the availability of prior knowledge, which improves the probability that the situation under investigation will be correctly identified and an optimal solution selected.

There is a danger here, too, of course. If the discovery team is too focused on prior knowledge, it may miss new or innovative opportunities. One of the ways that we can improve the discovery process with experience, but control the tendency to overweight experience when a new situation is encountered, is to use models to test our understanding of the problem and of our proposed solution.

The Role of Models

Trying to understand and manipulate the vast amount of information that constitutes the real world is a complex and sometimes impossible task. There is too much that must be understood and too much of that changes too rapidly to be assimilated. One of the most powerful tools we have for helping with this understanding, assimilation, and manipulation process is the concept of a *model*. Models allow us to represent the real world with a simplified alternative, created using a process called *abstraction*. Models typically either exclude sets of information that are not relevant to the purpose for which the model is constructed (this is a form of *partitioning*), or reduce the amount of detail that the information in the model represents (*simplification*). Some types of models may do both.

We should all be familiar with various types of models from common experirence. In many cases, we use models as a means of experimentation without having to make difficult, expensive, or dangerous changes to the real world. For instance, a model of a house can give a prospective buyer a much better idea of what it will be like to live in, than would a long, written description, and producing the model is much cheaper than building the house for real, only to find that it is unsuitable. Their general usefulness makes models commonplace in a wide variety of forms and with many purposes (see Table 6.1). In all cases, however, a model represents some aspects of reality that have been abstracted from the totality of the real world into a more readily understandable, or easier-to-use form.

Table 6.1 *Examples and Purposes of Common Types of Models*

Model	Purpose
A scale model of an airplane	To test the flight characteristics of the aircraft design, in a wind tunnel test. Although the model plane might not actually be able to fly, it is a sufficiently good representation of an airfoil that it can be used to assess expected behavior in flight.
A map of a subway train system	To enable passengers to find their way around town. The map does not maintain an accurate representation of distance, nor, necessarily, spatial relationships. It does, however, represent topological and connectivity information accurately and usefully.
A car's wiring diagram	To help mechanics and owners to trace and repair electrical faults. This is similar to the subway map example, although there might be a higher degree of correspondence to the actual physical layout of the wiring in the real world.
A profit-and-loss account	To show how the activities of a firm contributed to its overall profitability during a specific period. This may not, at first sight, look like a model, but we have actually substituted the numbers in the P&L statement for the real amounts of money that were collected or spent. This type of numeric model is among the most common types of abstract models in common use. Note that the model, as generally understood, contains no "hidden" information, even though there is explicit arithmetic relating different entries to each other. However the form of presentation (content and format), the information in the model adheres to a convention that is not directly inferred from the form of the model. Hence interpretation of the content of the model will

Table 6.1 *(Continued)*

Model	Purpose
	vary according to how well the underlying conventions are understood.
An office floor plan	To help anyone who needs to find their way around the office. Offices are actually complex, three-dimensional structures with many moveable (and often moving) parts. Their general layout usually remains fixed in two dimensions and it is unusual to need knowledge of either the third dimension (height) or the details of furniture, etc., in order to find one's way around. A two-dimensional representation of the main (fixed) features of the structure which is accurate as to their relative position and dimensions will therefore suffice as a guide.
An architectural model	To help the architect's clients to visualize the internal and external appearance of a building. This is a typical example of a scale model. Such models replicate the principle features and spatial relationships of the real world, but reduce both the dimensions and the levels of detail that are presented. Although scale models are common, their use is generally restricted to areas where scale factors do not influence that behavior of the topic being modeled. Thus an architectural model cannot usually be used to estimate the strength and quantity of the materials required to construct a building because these depend on properties that are not being modeled.
A recipe	To describe how to prepare a particular dish. This is an interesting example. A recipe models both a process (preparing the dish) and a deliverable (the dish itself, modeled as a combination of ingredients and the preparation process). In

(*Table continues on next page*)

Table 6.1 *(Continued)*

Model	Purpose
	theory, the syntax of a recipe is sufficient to generate the required result, even if the cook has never used the recipe before and has never eaten the resulting dish. Thus the semantics of the preparation process are well designed. However, it is not possible to infer the taste of the result (usually considered important in cooking) without information not contained in the model, so that the semantics of the model of the result are less well designed.
An organization chart	To show who reports to whom. This kind of model is a good example of the use of a stylized diagram to represent an already abstract structure. The relative positions of the boxes on the chart are used as metaphors for the reporting relationships between individuals. Here a spatial relationship (above/below) is being used to describe an organizational relationship (reports to). This use of a metaphor is also a very common feature of models and is especially useful in the models used by information systems developers.
An airline schedule	To assist prospective passengers to select the appropriate flight. This is an example of a model that replaces the time dimension with a physical layout metaphor. It also replaces actual spatial relationships (where places are in relationship to each other) with a much simpler relationship (connected pairs of route end-points).
A vacation tour itinerary	To describe and organize the components of a vacation. This is another interesting example. Although the itinerary has much in common with an airline schedule, it brings together a number of quite distinct sets of information. We have: sequence information (very important) describing

Table 6.1 *(Continued)*

Model	Purpose
	the order in which travel and stops occur; location information (also important) describing where the stops actually are; and absolute time and space relationships, describing when events must occur in specific places, all represented in a single model, usually as a single list of items. Note also that a model of an itinerary (such as we might generate for a travel agent's booking system) is not therefore the same as a travel model, which is what the itinerary represents. There are actually two levels of abstraction involved.
A budgeting spreadsheet	To forecast profitability under different assumptions of income and expenditure. Here is an example of a numeric model (like the P&L example above) but this time used to experiment with the effect of different assumptions on an expected, real-world outcome. Clearly we can't try out more than one set of assumptions in practice, so we must work with the abstract model instead.

To be useful, models need to have a purpose and some specific features:

- They need to be accurate representations of some aspects of the real world, even though they are not accurate representations of all aspects, so that we can recognize what it is that they are models of.
- They need to be derivable from the real-world situations that contain the aspects they represent in a repeatable and understandable fashion.
- It should be possible to manipulate them in ways that are useful analogs of real-world behaviors, so that we can use them to investigate the real world.

- The abstraction processes that are used to form a model, and the models that result, should be commonly understood by anyone who is knowledgeable about the subject matter of the model.

The *purpose* for which a model is constructed is often critical, because it determines the *content* of the model. A model should only contain things that contribute directly to its purpose. For instance, realistic cabin layouts in an aircraft model to be used for wind tunnel tests would be pointless. The work effort to produce them would be wasted.

It's not only the content of the model that is set by its purpose. We must also set the level of detail used to describe each part of the content. For instance, although a wiring diagram is likely to include colors for each wire, it will not specify color as exactly as a decorator's paint chart should.

Those who work with models use two technical terms—*granularity* and *specificity*—for these notions of the level of detail that a model contains. *Granularity* is the notion of *how many kinds of things* are specified in a model. The more granular the model, the more kinds of things it contains. *Specificity* is *how much detail* is recorded for each individual part of the model. The more specific the model, the more precisely each part is described.

Inventing models is, in general, an inexact science. Each model represents the real world in a particular way. It can use graphics, mathematical formulas, narrative, physical constructs, or analogies. A good model is very precise about its rules for representing the world, which is called its *syntax*. For instance, a subway map will represent each route using a different color line, and will draw these lines differently if they operate throughout the week, only at peak periods, or not during weekends. Models must also be precise about the meaning given to the components that represent real-world objects. This is called the model's *semantics*. To continue with the subway map example, readers must know that a *node* represents a station and that *lines* represent routes. If this basic meaning is missed, exact syntax will not be sufficient to convey the intended information.

To be useful, models must balance semantics (meaning) and syntax (construction rules). They must usually also balance understandability (which usually implies simplicity and a close correspondence to the real world) with power of manipulation (which often implies a high degree of abstraction). In general, the higher the degree of abstraction used to create a model, the harder it is to understand what the model represents. Thus a model car is recognizably a car, even though it may have no engine and many of the features of a car are represented only as icons, not as functions. On the other hand, Maxwell's equations for the electromagnetic field are not recognizable by many people as a model for the functioning of an electric motor or generator.

Models can represent any of three aspects of the real world:

1. As it is now—the *current* state;
2. As we would expect (or would like) the world to be—the *future* state;
3. How we intend it to be—usually a *transition* state (which may well be different from what we would like it to be, for all kinds of reasons.

It is often the time dimension that decides which state a model represents and the representation is likely to change over time. For instance, once a solution is built, its model obviously stops depicting an intention and instead describes the present—it changes from a future- or transition-state model to a current-state model. (The budget spreadsheet is a good example. A spreadsheet could include: last year's actual results [current state]; this year's forecasting model [future state]; or the actual allocated budget for the year [transition state and current state] at various times in its life cycle.)

It takes more than just elapsed time to change models from solution to environment. Some construction or implementation activity also has to take place so that the current state is modified. For instance, when an airline introduces a new route to its schedule, air and ground crews have to be informed and perhaps trained, and the schedule needs to be published and entered into the flight booking system. This work has to be done after the transition-state model (i.e., the new outline schedule) is built, and before it becomes the current state.

Using Models

Each type of model has a distinct purpose, that determines the level of detail represented in the model. A model abstracts only the necessary aspects of the real world, and presents these aspects clearly and precisely. A model may represent a view of the world as it is now, as it is expected to be, or as we intend to make it.

The initial key to good modeling is to get the purpose, level of detail, aspect depicted, and method of representation correct, or, in other words, to:

- Decide the purpose or objective of the model, including the aspects of the world that it will represent.
- Work out the level of abstraction needed.
- Build the model using the correct tools and techniques.
- Recognize that the model has reached the correct level of abstraction (granularity and/or specificity), and *stop building it*.

These are all technical processes. No account is necessarily taken of relevance. Thus it is possible to build technically correct models that do not represent anything in the real world. (You can easily draw a subway map for a city that has no subway system, for example.)

Two further keys to good model building are therefore concerned with:

1. Confirming that the model is relevant for its purpose; and
2. Bringing the model into effective use.

The ways that a model is confirmed and used can potentially lead to changing the levels of abstraction and style of representation from those demanded only by the model's original purpose or by purely technical considerations.

Using Models to Help with Developing Ideas

One of the general purposes of modeling is to test and make decisions more easily than would be possible without the model. For instance, architects will need to decide the appearance of a new house, and will produce a sketch of it to help in doing so. They will also decide the internal arrangement of rooms initially by making a rough sketch, and later by drawing-up a detailed scale plan. The architect will be able to visualize the house from the plan.

Unfortunately, the people who are going to live in the house won't have as much experience with house plans as their architect. They will need drawings of what the house will look like, or even possibly a scale model, in order to be able to have a useful discussion with the architect. Because they can't visualize as well (or in the same way) as the professional, the model that the architect builds must be geared toward their needs as well.

The final user of the model is the building firm. If they just got a scale model from the architect, the house might not end up being anything like the architect intended or the client wanted. A much more detailed set of architect's drawings is required, showing the services, and the specifications of all materials and fittings. The architect is responsible for ensuring that the scale plans, the drawings, and the detailed specifications all correspond with what the clients think they're getting.

The last key to effective modeling is therefore to remember who is going to use the model and to understand what they are going to use it for. Each user of the model may need different ways of representing the real world. The model developer has to ensure that the model can be understood by the eventual user, and also that it gives all necessary information to those who are going to develop the model further or to implement it back into the real world.

Models in Information Systems

Building information systems is similar to, but not identical with, the process of building a house (see Figure 6.1). The customer has a requirement that they attempt to articulate to an intermediary, who will translate the requirements into a set of specifications to be used by technically qualified practitioners who will build and deliver. Since the customer does not usually understand the complexities of the technologies that will be used to meet their requirements, some way must be found to ensure that what the technicians

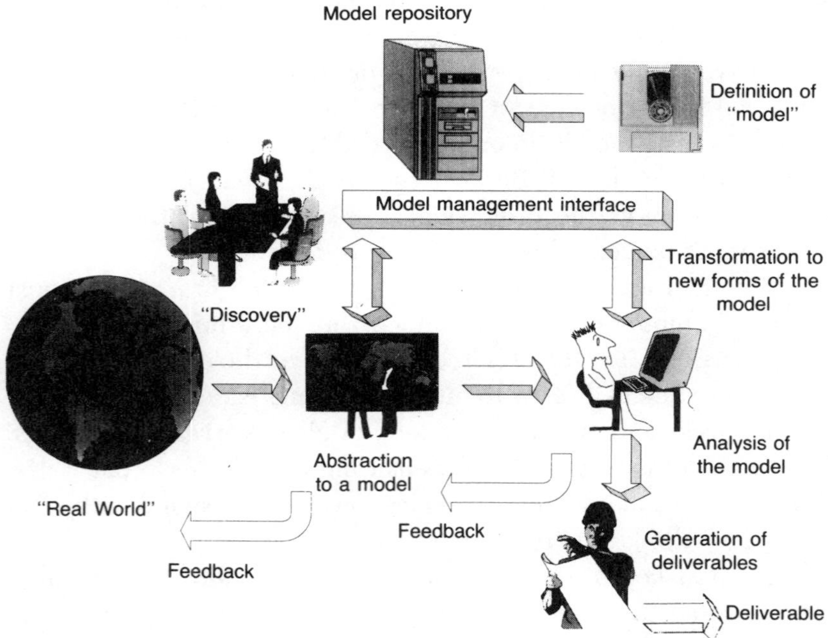

Figure 6.1 *The "modeling" cycle in information system development.*

build is what the customer wants. Waiting until the information system is finished and then trying it out is a costly and inefficient approach, since extensive rework may be necessary to match delivery to requirements. (This is analogous with building the house to see if it is what the client wants to live in.)

Instead, we need a way to build a model of the client's requirements that can be manipulated to generate the specifications from which the technicians will build the solution. This was the objective of the early proponents of structured methods. That the idea of using models is a good one has not really been questioned. Debate has centered around:

- What the models should contain;
- What they should look like;
- How they should be interpreted;
- Who should use them; and
- The degree to which they can be automated.

Many different forms of models have been proposed over the 20 years or so that structured methods have been in use. New forms are still being invented and introduced on a regular basis. In general, however, a small number of common model forms have emerged as the "standard" approach in each of the main IS development domains. It's important to remember, however, that the models are domain-specific and their form and meaning therefore varies according to the nature of the domain. Thus, models used to represent the requirements for real-time control systems have both different syntax and different semantics from models used to represent requirements for transaction-oriented business-support systems. Even when the form of the model (as represented by the types of diagram used) seems similar, the models may be very different.

Since we are concerned here only with developing business information systems, we will not look, in detail, at the model forms used in the other IS domains. Within our area of interest, models are normally used to represent:

- The strategy of an enterprise or strategic business unit and the factors that are critical to achieving the strategy;
- The organization and geographical location of the enterprise;
- How information is used by the enterprise and how that information is organized;
- How the main business processes of the enterprise operate and how they respond to external events;
- How these processes use information;
- How the enterprise organizes its information technology to support information systems development and operations;
- How information systems and the databases that they use are designed; and
- How these information systems and databases are implemented.

Table 6.2 shows the forms of models commonly used in each of these areas.

The above list is by no means comprehensive. In particular, the technology models and design and implementation models have many variants depending on the technologies being modeled. It is important, however, to remember the purpose of all of this modeling activity—to ensure that the information system that is delivered meets the requirements for functionality and usability set out by the customers for whom it was built. Insofar as the models listed above support that objective, the models are useful tools. If they do not support the objective effectively, their use is not justified.

Assisting with Transformation

As the models that we use move from a description of the current state, through transition, to a definition of the future state that we are trying to create, they undergo transformations. The modeling processes that we choose and the tools that we select to support them should make these transformations as easy and

Table 6.2 *Forms of Models Used by Information Systems Development*

Purpose of Model	Model Representation
Strategy	Decomposition diagram(s)
	Decision tables
	Budget spreadsheets
	Association matrix
	Ishikawa diagram
Organization and location	Organogram
	Organizational decomposition
	Network diagram
	Map
Data	Entity relationship diagram
	Data structure model
Processes	Context diagram
	Event matrix
	Data-flow diagram
	Process dependency diagram
	Work and document flow diagram
Process use of data	Entity model view
	Process vs. data-usage matrix
	Life-cycle diagram
	Entity life history
Information architecture	Network diagram
	Organogram
	Map
Application and database design	Structure chart
	Action diagram
	Procedure dependency diagram
	State transition diagram
	Dialog-flow diagram
	Screen and report layout
	Flow chart
	Data-structure diagram
	Database diagram

(*Table continues on next page*)

Table 6.2 *(Continued)*

Purpose of Model	Model Representation
Application and database implementation	Data definition language Data manipulation language Source code System control language

reliable as possible. We will want each transformation of our models to be:

- As automatic as is feasible, to minimize the amount of additional discovery or definition work required to complete it successfully.
- Reversible, so that, at a later date, we can recreate the requirements for which the application represents a solution. If this can't be done, we will have to retain both the requirements model and the solution model and keep them synchronized.

There will be at least four significant transformations required in the IS development-and-delivery process: (1) real world to problem model; (2) problem model to solution model; (3) solution model to implementable solution; and (4) implementable solution to real world.

Generating Deliverables

Our models can do us one final favor in supporting improved productivity and reduced cycle time. They can act as the repository of "content" from which we can generate the deliverables we require to meet the objectives of our project. Here again is a process that we would like to be as "automatic" as possible. When everything is in place in the model and appropriate levels of granularity and specificity have been reached, we should be able to "press a button" and have the deliverable generated for us without additional work effort.

How Much Process Management Is Needed?

If we have an effective, model-driven process that starts with a richly populated baseline that contains our past experience abstracted in model form, we should be able to complete the entire development-and-delivery process quickly and with a minimum of process-management "overhead." Since such overhead is not "value added" from the point of view of our project and its objectives (it can be argued that process management is only there to cope with our failure to predict completely the course of the project prior to its inception), we definitely want to minimize it without compromising our ability to manage the risk factors associated with uncertainty.

"Don't Do Anything More Often Than You Have To": Elimination of Unnecessary Rework

Eliminating unnecessary rework is a basic tenet of virtually all process-improvement approaches. Rework is not "value-added" activity in meeting a project's objectives and consumes resources that could be better used elsewhere. It also takes up elapsed time and may hold up other work, circumstances both which lengthen cycle times.

Categories of Rework

Virtually all rework is caused by various types of *defects*, resulting from four main sources:

1. **Defects due to process failures.** In general, this means we missed some essential work early in the process and, as a result, made assumptions that later proved to be false and must be reexamined. Alternatively, we may be doing the work in the wrong order, causing dependency-related delays as we wait for work products that should have been completed, but are not yet available. The more we can tailor the approach we use to the characteristics of the situation in which we are working, the less likely we are to get these kinds of process failures. Nevertheless, some of the work of the IS developer deals with discovery in the face of uncertainty, and we can never eliminate process failures entirely.
2. **Defects due to an incomplete initial baseline.** This category of rework occurs when we use resources to rediscover something we already know—but didn't know we knew. If we had efficient discovery processes, this might not be a significant problem, but too often the new discovery effort results in a worse answer than is already available. As we build-up the repository of prior knowledge, experience, and deliverables, the content of the initial baseline can provide an increasing proportion of each new project's required outputs. Eventually, as we have seen, it may be possible to have over 95 percent of the required output already available at the start of the project.
3. **Defects due to participant incompetence.** As the complexity of business problems and the technology that supports solutions increases, the sets of skills needed to address solution delivery grows in number and depth. It is not usually possible for individual developers to possess all of the required skills at the necessary levels of ability. Many defects result from the work of well-intentioned individuals who are not sufficiently well equipped to deal with the complexities of the situation in which they must work. Although better training and experience can help

to alleviate this problem, the long-term solution requires a move to better-defined, role-based project team assignments. This shift brings with it the need to develop and deploy adequate certification and performance-assessment processes, and to provide capability-development opportunities to developers to meet changing competency demands. It also implies significant shifts in recognition and reward systems, career path design, and organizational structures.

4. **Defects due to an inappropriate solution paradigm.** This category of rework occurs when the solution we deliver does not solve the business problem to which it is applied—whether or not it works. This is one of the most difficult categories to identify in classical development lifecycle processes, where customers only see the solution when it is "finished." Eliminating the category is dependent on improved requirements-discovery processes, which are difficult to implement and cannot guarantee success. Additional process- and people-related actions are needed to keep customers engaged in the development-and-delivery process so that early detection of solution failure can be achieved.

Eliminating Defects

Defects are an obvious source of rework, so eliminating them must be a priority. Note that we don't just want to *detect* and eliminate defects before our software is delivered to our customers. We want to *eliminate the source* of the defect, so that we don't have to do the detection and rectification work at all.[2] To eliminate the sources of defects, we must first find out what and where these sources are. Defect Source Analysis is an essential tool here, and eventually

[2]See, for example, Chaos: The Dollar Drain of IT Project Failures, by Jim Johnson. *Application Development Trends*, Vol. 2, No. 1, January 1995.

should be an automatic by-product of process management. Defect Source Analysis seeks to answer three questions:

1. **Where do defects get introduced?** If we know this, we can instrument those parts of the process that are most prone to be the source of defects, and focus improvement efforts there.
2. **Why do defects get introduced?** If we know this, we can select an appropriate defect-reduction strategy for each root cause and monitor its effectiveness.
3. **When do defects get found?** We want to catch any defects that we can't prevent as close as possible to the point at which they are created. This minimizes the probability that the defect will cause a "cascade" of additional rework. The discovery-lag metric measures the gap between the creation of a defect and the point at which it was finally detected.

Defect Source Analysis

Defect Source Analysis is the principal tool we use to do this. As each defect is detected (by whatever means) we will track it back to the point at which it was introduced, and then analyze why the defect arose. As we identify the sources of our defects we can take steps to eliminate these sources, thereby eliminating the defects.

We can do some additional improvement-focused analysis at the same time. If our detection methods are effective, they should catch defects very close to their points-of-origin. This will reduce the rework cost of the defect while we are attacking its source, and will improve our elimination effectiveness for defects whose source we cannot remove (unfortunately, there are some of these, as shall be shown). By recording the time lag between the point of introduction of a defect and the point of detection, we can create a detection-effectiveness metric, based on the "defect-discovery lag." We will want the recorded value of this metric to reduce (indicating a shorter detection lag) as our defect source analysis proceeds.

In traditional software-development processes, most defects get detected during the testing process, after considerable effort had been expended in designing and developing them.[3] Significant amounts of additional time and effort must then be expended to correct the identified defects, and the correction and retesting processes themselves may not be defect-free. In some cases, there seems to be a minimum level of defects that we cannot get below. Defect-Source Analysis and an active program of defect source elimination can reduce this minimum.

Potential for Reusability

One of the most significant potential areas for reducing rework is to reuse existing work (which represents a "sunk" resource cost). As we noted above, the potential to do so may approach or exceed 95 percent in some areas, and is almost always greater than is actually achieved. Reuse is, however, not "free." IS organizations pursuing a reuse strategy must answer at least the following two questions:

1. **What is "reusable"?** Actually, the answer is less important than the existence of a consistent process for getting an answer—but such a process is essential.
2. **How do you know when you've got a reusable component?** This is actually a more difficult question. Repositories of reusable components are an infant technology at any level above module source code, and require investment to create useful content before they become attractive to use.

Reuse is also more than just a technology issue. Processes must be adjusted to take account of component reuse. Recognition-and-

[3] It has been a common observation among the pioneers of improved software development processes that requirements analysis really starts during the user-testing process. This is the first time that real customers get to see what has been developed for them. They don't usually like it much.

reward systems must be adjusted to promote reuse, and to reward those who create and employ reusable components. This implies considerable change in working practices and a significant investment in infrastructure technology.

Reuse of software components and design ideas has, of course, been going on to some degree for many years. Most such reuse occurs at a relatively low level (typically small sections of program code), but there have been many attempts to promote reuse of larger and more abstract components, such as complete design specifications. These attempts have met with only limited success. Research at IBM's Center of Excellence in Reuse in Toronto, Canada, has shown that there is a plateau in the amount of reusable content in software at about the 30 percent to 35 percent level.[4]

There is a probable explanation for this relatively low figure. In order to reuse a component you must:

- Know that it exists and where it can be found;
- Be able to recognize that it will do the job that you require with less effort than it would take to develop a specific new component; and
- Be able to afford the components that you find.

If components are not adequately labeled, the effort required to find and evaluate a suitable example can exceed the benefits that can accrue from eliminating the development work that would otherwise be required.

This labeling requirement is a considerable challenge, because it requires additional effort on the part of the component developers. Components must be labeled both with a clear description of the intended use of the component and with guidelines that try to anticipate the range of situations for which the component should also be considered.

Unless component developers are given incentives to do this

[4]Reported in a presentation made by IBM to the E&Y Carolinas IS Quality program meeting, Charlotte, North Carolina, July 1994.

labeling, component reuse will be limited to those examples where the usage is obvious. These will typically be small code modules of limited utility and scope.

Even when components are well labeled initially, it is rare that subsequent uses of a component exactly match the original intent of the first developers. Each reuse therefore needs to be recorded, so that a richer set of possible usese can be built-up over time. However, this "close but not exact" usage history means that the original label becomes "blurred" as successive reuse occurs.

Eventually, there is a danger that the "envelope of expected utility"—the range of situations for which the component appears to be a suitable match—will expand too far and the component will become a source of defects in some "edge-of-the-envelope" use. If we are not careful, this may cause the component to be marked as defective for *all* uses, removing it from consideration in situations where it should still be available.

This "entropic degradation" of reusable components is the second major barrier (after effective initial labeling) to pushing the reuse content above the observed plateau level.

Roles, Competencies, and Getting the Right People for the Job

As we have seen, the range of competencies required to develop information systems is growing and is already large. It is tempting to address the problems of sustained high performance by hiring only multi-skilled, highly competent people, who already have the range of skills required. With this approach, no matter what range of skills required for a project, we will always have "the right people" available and resource allocation and scheduling will be simplified.

There are dangers, however, with this "renaissance person" approach. First, there are very few people available who are really as good as we would need. They are hard to find, expensive to hire, and difficult to keep. Companies that adopt this strategy may find themselves in a bidding war with their competitors for a small pool of talent available. Second, even such highly talented people find it difficult to stay current with all the developments in process and technology.

If we can't depend on all of our staff knowing everything we need them to know, what can we do? The obvious alternative is to have the required skills spread over more people, and blend them together in a "cross-functional" team. This trades-off the simpler resource allocation of the renaissance person model with the more realistic development of specific competencies within individuals. Scheduling is harder, and we have to know which roles require what skills, but at least we have a shot a building-up the necessary competencies among the people we can actually find, hire, and hope to keep.

We also have to address the fact that not everyone in the IS organization will be equally skilled and experienced at any given time. In any given team we will inevitably have a mixture of new, somewhat experienced, and (hopefully) very experienced staff. This range of abilities further pushes the need to understand the competency requirements of our project work and the corresponding level-of-skill impact on assigned roles and tasks. The better we get at assigning work to staff with appropriate levels of skill and experience, the fewer competency-related defects we will get. Where competency gaps exist that cannot be filled with better resource allocation, we can, at least, adjust schedule and cost estimates to reflect this reality, and include appropriate risk-management activity.

Plan for the Rework You Know Is Inevitable

Even if we eliminate all of the rework due to defects, we can't get rid of all rework. As we saw in Chapter 4, requirements analysis will always demand that we be prepared to do some things several times, to be sure that we have everything as right as possible, before we proceed to a solution. The key, however, is *to be prepared*. If we know we are going to apply the three-iterations rule, we should *plan* to do so—not have it happen as a surprise.

"Do as Much as You Can at Once": Increased Parallel Execution

There is a famous example of the power of parallel execution to reduce cycle times, using the process of building a house as an example.[5] For most people, the building of a house is a prolonged process that they feel fortunate to have accomplished if completed within 90 days. It can often take much longer. There are usually anywhere from four or five to perhaps as many as 20 people involved. The total labor content varies a great deal with house size, floor plan, and area of the country, but most houses take between 3,000 and 10,000 hours of effort to build. So, just *how fast* could a real house be built?

The School of Construction Engineering at the University of Illinois decided to find out. They analyzed the house-building process in minute detail and identified the critical work paths. They then attacked each element of the critical path, in turn, until they could not get further efficiency improvements. When they had the most efficient process possible, they assembled the necessary resources and trained everyone who would be involved. Then they practiced the process several times. Finally, they really built the house, and made a videotape of the entire process with a visible timeline as a part of the recording. How long did it take, and how many people were involved? Just over four hours with more than 800 people. That's a total of about 3,500 construction hours for a real house that would have passed the code inspection in the area where it was built.

[5] University of Illinois, School of Construction Engineering, 1990.

Most people don't believe these numbers at first, but the videotape can be rented and watched in its entirety (there is also a shorter "highlights" version) as dramatic proof of what can be achieved.

There are critical factors required to achieve this degree of cycle time compression. Let's see what lessons can be learned from them.

- The project planners researched and understood all of the critical dependencies in the work. For instance, it was clear that the footings for the foundations had to be in place and secure before the foundation slab was poured or the walls erected. Other dependencies were less clear and were examined closely to see if they could be removed. As a result of this examination, many apparently fixed constraints were eliminated.
- A number of seemingly irreducible time periods were removed or reduced by changing either the tools and materials used or the work processes involved. For example, the substitution of a special, fast-setting cement to replace the regular concrete mix allowed the "curing" time for the footings and foundation slab to be reduced from 30 hours to 45 minutes.
- The members of the project team were all given clear roles and responsibilities and then allowed to practice them until they were confident, individually and as a team, that they knew what to do and how to do it.
- There was consistent and effective direction, from the project managers at all levels, throughout the construction process. Individual team leaders knew their team's objectives in detail as well as their place in the whole process. Process managers knew what the teams had to accomplish and by when, so they could keep track of progress. The overall project manager had a master timeline to work to, so that he could adjust the "pool" resources to account for any variations from the ideal plan.

We can learn a lot from this example. Even conceding that this is not a good way to build every house, we can still see a graphic demonstration of the possibilities inherent in innovative thinking, excellent planning, and training, and a high degree of parallelism in the work plan.[6] Although increased parallel working is principally a strategy for reducing the elapsed time on projects, two side-effects of reduced elapsed time also have direct productivity contributions:

1. Some process-management tasks require resources that are related to the duration of the project rather than to the work to be performed. Reducing the duration reduces the resources required for these tasks.
2. As more work is carried out in parallel, the exchange of available information that is now possible reduces the probability that defects will be missed and allows corrective action to be taken earlier than might otherwise occur, reducing rework.

Balancing these gains, however, are a number of issues that must be addressed.

- **Knowing the "right order" in which to do things.** Although most of the dependencies in a compressed life cycle are "finish/finish," there is still a "preferred order" for most of the work and a few things that must be done in the right order to avoid significant rework.
- **Knowledge coordination and the challenge of doing everything at once.** As elapsed time for the work decreases and the number of parallel tasks increases, the need to

[6]It probably isn't. The team spent nearly 12,000 additional hours practicing the process they would use before starting the actual construction. They would probably have had to practice again before building another, although less practice would have been required. They would also have had to rest for a while between houses. Overall, their productivity would not have been much better than that of the regular process, although the cycle time per house would still have been a little better.

keep everyone involved up-to-date on issues, progress, and status grows rapidly. Conventional knowledge-coordination processes cannot cope with very high levels of parallelism, and quickly become bottlenecks, or are ignored, raising the risks of process failure. New processes and practices are required and must be managed.

- **Project management and control issues.** Similar issues relate to the management and control of the project. As elapsed times reduce, the "slack" available to project managers within which to adjust the project schedule to accommodate unplanned work is rapidly eliminated. Static project-management models quickly fail to provide adequate control at an economic cost. New management processes and skills are required.

These issues may require additional resources for the reduced duration of the project, eroding some of the productivity gains.

"Supply and Use the Right Processes and Tools"

Drowning in the Seas of Inadequate Automation

There is no shortage of tools available to the IS practitioner. The database of tool-related knowledge that we maintain, to track what is available for our practitioners, contains well over 1,200 entries and grows at a rate of about 10 new entries and 40 updates per month. The problem lies in providing a set of tools that work together effectively, that actually support the IS development-and-delivery process well enough to be worth the effort of learning to use them. Increasingly, the effective deployment of tools depends on issues such as:

- Establishing a stable and effective infrastructure that supports tool usage;

- Having processes that are tuned to be effective when supported with specific tools; and
- Educating staff to be aware of what tools are available, what they can do, and what they should be used for.

Creating an effective group of "tool users" requires both substantial initial investment and adequate sustaining engineering to keep the tools current with evolving needs. Unless the processes that the tools support are established and understood, the tools will fail, or at best, be reduced in effectiveness. Unless a sufficient number of people will benefit from the tools, insufficient expertise will be developed and the tools will fail or be ineffective. Unless the tools portfolio is kept relevant and up-to-date, tools will fall into disuse. Tools require integration and support in exactly the same way that business applications do.

An Architecture for Organizing Tools

To provide a sense of the range and scope of the tools needed by a high-performing applications development-and-delivery group, we have developed a high-level architecture that organizes the tools into seven functionally related "tool kits" and three kinds of repositories (see Figure 6.2).

1. **Process knowledge management (alias methodology engineering).** This is the set of tools we use to describe, organize, and document the processes that define the way the IS organization does its work. Think of it as the repository of everything the IS organization knows how to do, organized so that it can be used to create specialized project workplans, as required.
2. **Knowledge management.** This tool kit lets us collect, organize, and deploy the collective experience of the IS organization and any external sources of best practices that we may choose to use. It ensures that anything important or useful that is known to anyone is available to everyone else who might need it.

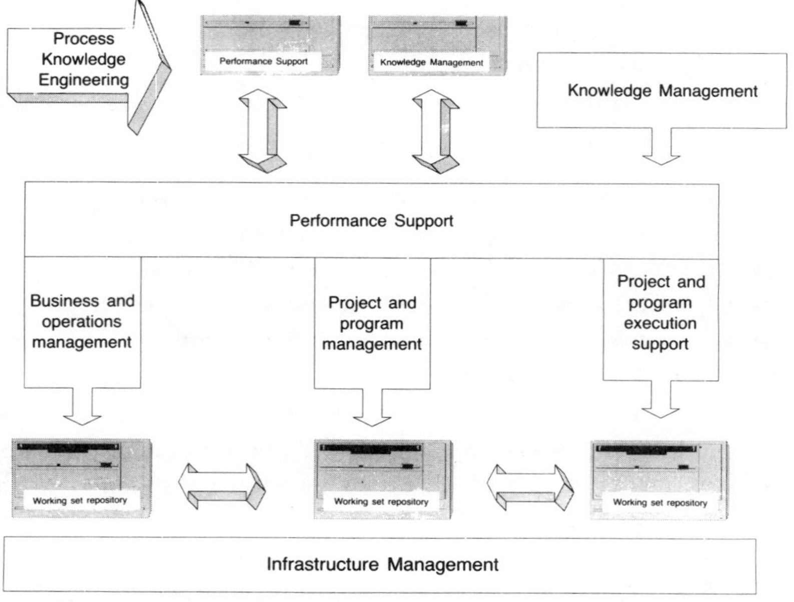

Figure 6.2 *An architecture for organizing the tools that support the IS development-and-delivery process.*

3. **Business operations support.** These are the tools that let us run the IS development-and-delivery process as a business.
4. **Program and project management.** This tool kit lets our program and project managers structure and plan the work of the IS organization, track progress and adjust plans to match actual experience, diagnose potential problems, measure performance, assess status, and report to sponsors.
5. **Service delivery.** These are the tools that the IS organization uses to actually build and deploy information systems that support real business processes.
6. **Performance support.** This tool kit provides the passive and active help needed by IS staff to maintain peak levels of performance and continuously improve competencies.

7. **Infrastructure management.** This tool kit supports the management, administration, and operation of the infrastructure used by the IS organization.

We also have three kinds of repositories in the architecture:

1. **Working-set repositories.** These are the databases, files, and documents that represent work in progress during a project. The content is typically incomplete or changing rapidly, so we do not yet want to incorporate it into the more stable knowledge bases.
2. **Process-knowledge repositories.** These are the knowledge bases that hold the specialized knowledge related to IS processes and their related performance support. Although they are really just part of the overall knowledge environment, we manage them separately because of the requirements to use the content to drive project structure and planning processes.
3. **Knowledge repositories.** These are the main knowledge bases for examples, best practices, experiential material, and outside reference sources.

Within this architecture, specific tools and supporting technologies can be identified according to the processes they support and the individuals and groups at which they are targeted. Table 6.3 lists some of the typical types of tool found in each tool kit.

Examples of Value-Added Tools

In general, we can also distinguish three target groups for the types of tools we provide:

1. Tools for individuals, such as time reporting, model building, testing, or documentation.
2. Tools for teams, such as status reporting, process management, or work-flow management repositories, and group discussion facilities.

Table 6.3 *Examples of Types of Tools Needed by the High-Performing IS Organization*

Tool Kit	Example Tool Type
Process-knowledge management	Process specification and specialization
Knowledge management	Knowledge acquisition and classification
	Knowledge content analysis
	Knowledge association analysis
	Knowledge-usage analysis
	Knowledge retrieval
	Information alerts and broadcasts
Business operations support	Resource management
	Competency model and staff development
	Certification and training management
	Plans and budgets
	Financial reporting and analysis
	Operational measures and effectiveness analysis
Program and project management	Program and project design
	Estimation and scheduling
	Economic analysis and reporting
	Time and cost capture, analysis, and reporting
	Operational measures and effectiveness analysis
	Project process simulation
	Process management and reporting
	Team communication and collaboration
Service delivery	Discovery support
	Modeling and model analysis
	Model transformation
	Design and performance simulation
	Work-product management and version control
	Testing and verification
	Deliverable generation, version control and configuration management
	Work-flow management

Table 6.3 *(Continued)*

Tool Kit	Example Tool Type
Performance support	Help in context Wizards and cue cards Smart advisors
Infrastructure management	Performance modeling and simulation Capacity planning Backup and recovery

3. Tools for everyone, such as e-mail, various kinds of performance support, or broadcast communications.

All three types exist in each of the seven segments of the architecture. In many cases, the same type of tool can be used in more than one mode.

Note that we have specified types of tools, *not products*. The best product in each category will change over time. More important than a specific product selection is a set of architectural principles that can be applied to select and integrate the best product available from time to time.

Catalog of Acceleration Practices

So put me on a highway and show me a sign. Let's take it to the limit one more time.[1]

Accelerators and How to Use Them

What Is an Accelerator?

In our research, an *accelerator* was any commonly used practice that consistently *reduced* the cycle time of a process to which it was applied. We looked for practices that were used successfully by more than one organization, to reduce the organizational and cultural bias in the results (although we acknowledge that some bias remains). We also looked for practices that were successful when repeated by the same or different teams in multiple organizations, reducing the bias that results from only considering compliant problems or from the "A-team" effect.

Provenance and Cautions

The Ernst & Young IS Development and Delivery Process Accelerators Ressearch program, started in 1988, is a continuing, long-term program to improve the efficiency of E&Y's service delivery process for IS development and delivery. It involves measurement and examination of E&Y and client IS development-and-delivery processes and experimentation with innovative process management, process execution, organization, and technology. It has the objective, by the end of 1997, to develop an IS development-and-delivery process that will support a cycle time of less than 30 days for any information systems development-and-delivery requirement.

[1]Lyric from the track "Take It to the Limit," by the rock band "The Eagles." From the album "On the Border," written by R. Meisner, D. Henley, and G. Frey. Copyright 1984, WB Music Corp./Kicking Bear Music ASCAP.

So far the research program has collected data on some 800 projects—450 from E&Y engagements and 350 from clients where there was no E&Y participation in the project. In addition, it has recently formed links with the U.S. chapter of International Function Point Users Group (IFPUG) (now renamed the Association for Software Management—ASM) to share performance metrics.

The *IT Thought Leadership Program* was a two-year, multi-client research program (1992–1994) aimed at identifying and sharing best practices among approximately 20 of the leading exponents of IS performance in the United States and Europe. The program sponsored action groups focusing on specific areas of practice sharing (Reskilling, Transition Management, Measurement, and Acceleration).

The *Carolinas Information Services Quality Program* is an Ernst & Young-sponsored, multi-client program servicing education, practice-sharing, and peer group networking for IS executives from businesses based in the Carolinas. Members subscribe annually to participate in a series of six one-day meetings, held in Charlotte, North Carolina, that address topics of importance to the continuing success of information services in creating and sustaining business value. Each member of the program sends a small group of participants to each meeting, typically senior IS executives and their immediate reports. At least one meeting in each program is aimed at the participation of the CIOs themselves.

The IT Thought Leadership Program overall membership and Acceleration Action Group participant organizations are listed in Appendix 1. The Carolinas IS Quality Program participant organizations and guests are listed in Appendix 2. Other data sources (E&Y engagements, non-client contacts, sources of correspondence, other research efforts, etc.), are listed in Appendix 3.

Each acceleration practice identified by the research is listed and described in this chapter. For each practice, we also describe:

- The organizations who use it (this may not be an exhaustive list);
- The objectives that are associated with the practice;

- The expected effect of successful implementation of the practice;
- The observed effects, where we have been able to quantify them;
- Which combination of practices seems to work best;
- Any comments that are associated with a practice; and
- Useful references and additional sources for the practice, if any.

In total, we identified over 60 individual practices in use among the study participants, but, on closer analysis, many of these were so similar that we were able to group them into a much smaller number of practices, which are described in this chapter. Many practices, despite the fact that they have different names, are really just flavors of the same fundamental ideas.

Accelerator 1. Migrate Routine or Repetitive Work into Infrastructure.

Description: Create a development support infrastructure that allows for the automation of routine administrative and development process tasks such as reporting, time recording, message broadcast, work assignment, and issue management.

Used by: Ameritech
E&Y LLP
Eli Lilly
IBM
Owens Corning Fiberglass

Used for: Reduction of effort required to support development process execution, project administration, and project management.

Expected Effects: Reduce process management overheads and effort by 15 percent to 30 percent, depending on the current baseline process efficiency.

Observed Effects: Initial reductions will be offset by learning curve and technology implementation issues. Net gains observed to be in the range of 12–20 percent in the first year, 25–40 percent in year 2. Improvements seem to be sustainable.

Combine with: High-Performance Development Environments (HPDE), Process Measurement.

Comments: Most IT processes can be assisted by effective infrastructure, even if full automation is not a feasible option. Justifying the infrastructure investment can, however, be difficult, and innovative funding and cost-justification models are emerging in response to the need to fund large-scale, long-term infrastructure development and deployment.

Additional References

Merlyn, V. P., & Parkinson, J. S. (1994). *Development Effectiveness: Strategies for IS Organizational Transition.* New York: John Wiley & Sons.

Boddie, J. (1993). *The Information Asset: Rational DP Funding and Other Radical Notions.* Englewood Cliffs, NJ: Yourdon Press.

McKay, D. T., & Brockway, D. W. (1989). *Building I/T Infrastructure for the 1990s. Stage by Stage* (Nolan Norton & Company).

The Role and Value of Information Technology Infrastructure: Some Empirical Observations. Center for Information Systems Research Working Paper No. 240, May 1992.

Sassone, P. G. (1987). Cost–Benefit Methodology for Office Systems. *ACM Transactions on Office Information Systems,* 5(3), 273–289.

Accelerator 2. Work Elimination through Process Specialization

Description: Provide an approach and tools that support the design of projects in which all planned work is attributable to efficient discovery, the development of a required deliverable, necessary option analysis, or risk management.

Used by: Ameritech
Apple
AT&T
Citizens' Coke & Gas
Corning
E&Y LLP
Grumman Data Systems
Hewlett Packard
Nestle SA
Operational Development Agency
Society Corp.
South Carolina Electric & Gas
Wachovia Financial Services

Used for: Design of projects that have no unnecessary planned effort. Techniques are provided that allow work-plan optimization both within and between projects from a variety of optimization objectives. Adopting this acceleration practice is usually an initial stage in moving to dynamic process management.

Expected Effects: Reduction of 35 percent in resources required for a project via elimination of all unnecessary and non-value-added work.

Observed Effects: Average planned project resource estimates decreased by 24 percent. Actual project out-turn reduced by an average of 16 percent. Only a very small percentage of projects are larger in estimate when planned this way, usually reflecting overly optimistic assumptions on the part of estimators using nonspecialized methods.

Combine with: HPDE and Process Mechanization.

Comments: Not necessarily a support mechanism for cycle time reduction, since the focus is on resource consumption, but the average project elapsed time is also down by about 20 percent, partly due to decreases in the work content of projects, leading to reduced duration.

The focus of this accelerator remains process efficiency. There is a secondary focus on project management effectiveness and on the effectiveness of related project support processes.

Additional References: This is a new area of investigation, with little literature available beyond specialized internal material from the few organizations who have put these ideas into effect. See, for example:

The Ernst & Young Navigator Systems Series, Version 2.1 Overview Monograph, Copyright 1994 Ernst & Young International. Available from Ernst & Young LLP Center for Business Transformation, 104 Decker Court, Irving TX 75062.

Accelerator 3. Self-Managed Teams

Description: Provide teams with a set of general but clear statements of objectives for their work, an optimization objective, and a set of defined constraints within which to operate. Allow the teams to plan in detail how to achieve their objectives.

Used by: E&Y LLP
Eli Lilly
Hewlett Packard

McDonald's
Xerox

Used for: Move routine decision-making closer to those involved with the decision point to improve cycle time. Allow teams to modify the process and use of technology to speed delivery.

Expected Effects: Shorter decision cycles. Fewer technology-related process failures resulting from enforced use of inappropriate technology. Reduced overall cycle times. Improved participant satisfaction, hence improved quality of outputs.

Observed Effects: In almost all cases there is an initial period of confusion and consequent loss of productivity as teams test the boundaries of their ability to act in a self-managed fashion. Potential gains are only realized after a team and its sponsors have discovered a successful operating model and both become comfortable with the boundaries of empowerment.

Combine with: Technology Enablers, Performance Support.

Comments: Note that these teams are *not* self-directed. The approach is most effective when clear objectives and constraints are set and team is allowed to operate freely within these. Team can, of course, challenge these constraints but cannot override them without external sanction. It may be necessary to adjust team composition if dysfunctional authority-related processes emerge or dominant individuals do not allow the team to operate effectively.

Additional References: There is an extensive literature on self-directed, high-performing teams, a selection of which is listed here.

Byham, W. C., with Cox, J. (1988). *Zapp! The Lightning of Empowerment.* New York: Fawcett Columbine.

Covey, S. R. (1989). *The 7 Habits of Highly Effective People.* New York: Simon & Schuster.

Fisher, K. (1993). *Leading Self-Directed Work Teams.* New York: McGraw-Hill.

Hess, K. (Ed.) (1987). *Creating the High-Performance Team.* New York: John Wiley & Sons.

Katzenbach, J. R., & Smith, D. K. (1993). *The Wisdom of Teams: Creating the High Performance Organization.* Boston: Harvard Business School Press.

Kayser, T. A. (1990). *Mining Group Gold.* El Segundo, CA: Serif Publishing.

Wheatly, M. J. (1992). *Leadership and the New Science.* San Francisco: Berrett-Koehler.

Accelerator 4. Component Reuse: Using the "Builders & Buyers" Model

Description: Create a reuse strategy that assigns specific resources to build and maintain reusable components (builders), and make them available to a larger group of application developers (buyers). Give both groups incentive toward the desired component reuse behavior, by rewarding both the most prolific builders of useful components and the most frequent consumers.

Used by: American Express TRS
Ameritech
Apple
Citizens' Coke & Gas
Coca-Cola Consolidated
E&Y LLP
Eli Lilly
Farmers Insurance
IBM
Owens-Corning Fiberglass
R.J. Reynolds
Society Corp.
Sun Microsystems
Xerox

Used for: Focus attention of developers on building useful common design-level and code-level components. Reward builders for the extent of reuse made of their contributions. Reward buyers for using available components. Encourage builder-buyer dialogs to identify additional reuse opportunities.

Expected Effects: Potential reuse levels of 95 percent or more exist. Initial targets of around 60 percent reuse in overall application image (including database and transaction-monitoring components) are common, with in excess of 40 percent targets set for developed code.

Observed Effects: Levels of reuse up from around 7 percent (common baselines are between 3 percent and 8 percent) to an average of about 30 percent in the developed code components of an application.

Combine with: Improved Infrastructure. HPDE and Process Mechanization. Coaching on Reuse.

Comments: Some of the benefit seems to be the result of better housekeeping processes and improved infrastructure provision and management practices. Actual levels of overall reuse are often masked by issues of terminology definition and measurement practices. The observed trends, however, are encouraging. Lack of an effective repository technology is a limitation. Knowledge Coordination processes are failing to act as an adequate substitute. The problems remain of correctly identifying the contact within which a component can be safely reused.

Additional References: There is an extensive literature on reuse, much of which focuses on the use of Object Oriented (OO) approaches to improved reuse. While we have seen significant gains through the use of OO technologies, we have seen equally impressive gains in component reuse in traditional, non-OO technologies. See, for example:

Martin, C., & Apfelbaum, H. (1994). Bridging the Gap between BPR Expectation, Reality of Implementation. *Application Development Trends, 1(9)*, 46–52.

Accelerator 5. Coaching by Experts

Description: Provide "process coaches" for small groups or individuals with little or no experience in the required working practices and technologies used by the IS organization, in order to accelerate learning and promote the rapid take-up and consistent use of best practices.

Used by: Alcon Laboratories
E&Y LLP
Hewlett Packard
IBM
Southern California Gas

Used for: Improved initial learning and rapid competency development in inexperienced trainees or in staff switching to new competencies.

Expected Effects: Reduction in learning curve effects and rapid institutionalization of best practices. Decrease in errors related to lack of experience. Improved early productivity in new staff or in staff faced with the adoption and use of unfamiliar technologies.

Observed Effects: Reduction in initial learning time from around 12 to under 3 months. Earlier achievement of useful competency, performance levels, and ability to work unsupervised. Dramatic reduction in defects related to lack of experience.

Combine with: HPDE. Component Reuse. Economies-of-scope.

Comments: Lack of qualified and capable coaches may be an issue. Failures in the coaching model are often attributable to the "coaching by quarterbacks" phenomenon in which the assigned coaches become frustrated at the learning pace of their trainees and intervene to perform the work themselves. This destroys almost all of the benefit to the trainee. Identifying and developing effective coaching behavior may be difficult in some organizations where the culture does not value this competency.

Accelerator 6. Economies-of-Scope

Description: Invest in achieving excellence in a small range of processes, problem domains, and technologies, rather than trying to be the best at everything.

Used by: E&Y LLP
IBM
Sapient

Used for: Development of a narrow range of competencies that can be performed to very high and consistent levels of productivity and quality. Narrowing of infrastructure focus to permit investment in a high-capability, sophisticated support environment.

Expected Effects: Improved productivity and quality levels through higher practitioner competency and more extensive reuse opportunities.

Observed Effects: Early results indicate a 50 percent reduction in cycle time once learning curve and infrastructure integration issues have been addressed. The ability to retain staff who work in a consistent and self-improving process appears to account for a great deal of the initial gains.

Combine with: Migration of Work into Infrastructure. Component Reuse; HPDE. Coaching by Experts.

Comments: Picking the right set of specializations to focus on is a critical success factor. However, given the need to achieve a critical mass of resources to develop and maintain high levels of expertise, only very large organizations can expect to support more than a handful of areas at the required levels of sustained high performance. Most companies will need more than these competencies to be available, at least through the transition period and probably thereafter.

To meet these additional needs, the IS organization must seek out and develop effective partnerships with external vendors and service providers who can provide the sustained levels of high performance required in areas that are not among the selected core competencies. This often implies that the IS organization must also learn new partnering and partnership behavior skills.

Additional References: There are a small number of interesting references to follow-up, since this is a new development for most IS organizations. For an excellent treatment of best practices for the IS organization in forming effefctive partnerships with business customers and others, see:

Henderson, J. C. (1990). *Plugging into Strategic Partnerships: The Critical IS Connection. Sloan Management Review, 31(3),* 7–18.

Olsen, D. (1993). *Exploiting Chaos.* VNR Computer Library. New York: Van Nostrand Reinhold.

Weinberg, G. M. (1988). *Rethinking Systems Analysis and Design.* New York: Dorset House.

Accelerator 7. High-Participation-Intensity Discovery Processes: Timebox, SWAT Teams, JAD, RAD

Description: Use facilitated workshops and group discovery processes that involve relatively large numbers of people (10–30), for short periods of time (1–6 weeks), to define and agree on requirements and confirm critical design parameters.

Used by: Ameritech
AT&T
Burlington Industries
Citizens' Coke & Gas
Coca-Cola Consolidated
E&Y LLP
Eastman Kodak
Eli Lilly
First Direct Bank Ltd.
First Union Bank
National City Bank
Owens Corning Fiberglass
Pacific Gas & Electric
R.J. Reynolds
Sara Lee Hosiery
Sonoco
South Carolina Electric & Gas
Springs Industries
USAA Group
Wachovia Financial Services
Xerox

Used for: Shorten cycle time by involving the key decision-making or influence-holding participants from all impacted business constituencies in the requirements discovery-and-solution design process.

Expected Effects: Obtain rapid consensus on scope and content or a clear indication that such agreement is not possible and thus that the problem scope or business case must be restated. There should be fewer missed requirements. There should be reduced rework from missed or misstated requirements. There should be improved acceptance of the proposed solution from customers. Fewer technology mismatches should occur.

Observed Effects: There is good and widespread anecdotal and some good quantitative research evidence to support claims for improved productivity and forced cycle time compression. Results are only positive for the right kind of problem/solution/skills mix.

Combine with: HPDE, Cross-Functional Teams.

Comments: This accelerator can also be used to select and customize purchased software and third-party packages. User involvement creates a better appreciation of the true costs of purchased software integration and the real gap between the purchased process and the current state.

Care needs to be taken to manage scope when there are many participants involved in requirements discovery. Increased participation can also slow initial problem definition and scope agreement.

Success is critically affected by the availability of experienced facilitators and of suitable infrastructure/environment to support the process. It is also essential to have the right blend of participation. As we were told by many of the organizations using the practice, "You only want participants who are too busy to attend." They are the ones who know what really goes on, because they are actually doing the work.

We have also seen the development of a "second-generation" process among those organizations who have used JAD-based techniques for several years. Early practitioners recommended small groups (typically 8 to 12 participants) and short sessions (less than a week). This limited the size and impact of the problems that could be addressed. As re-engineering has de-layered companies, more participants are required to get the necessary coverage, and systems tend to cross many organizational boundaries. In response, leading companies now include larger groups (up to perhaps 40 people) and work for longer periods (up to 6 weeks) to achieve an effective requirements definition and initial solution design.

Additional References: There is an extensive literature on these approaches and many commercial sources for process outlines, facilitator training, and techniques and tools. See, for example:

Andrews, D. C., & Leventhal, N. S. (1993). *Fusion*. Englewood Cliffs, NJ: Yourdon Press.

August, J. H. (1991). *Joint Application Design*. Englewood Cliffs, NJ: Yourdon Press.

Bouldin, B. (1989). *Agents of Change*. Englewood Cliffs, NJ: Yourdon Press.

Kerr, J., and Hunter, R. (1994). *Inside RAD*. New York: McGraw-Hill.

Accelerator 8. Work-Flow Management

Description: Use specialized process-management tools to ensure that the flow of work to developers is optimized (with the most important remaining task always presented to the next available qualified resource), and the overall work flow is balanced to match available people and skills.

Used by: Apple
E&Y LLP
R.J. Reynolds
Springs Industries

Used for: Provide a more appropriate scheduling paradigm for the flow of work into and through complex, interdependent IT processes and project work flows.

Expected Effects: Reduced scheduling- and precedence-related delays due to missing or out-of-sequence deliverables and work products. Fewer dependencies on critical resources.

Observed Effects: Learning curve effects and distrust of the scheduling tools can distort the expected savings. The more rigorous problem definition required to fully implement this approach can bring to the surface additional issues that are themselves sources of delay.

Combine with: Requirements-Discovery Processes. Cross-Functional Teams. High-Performance Development Environment (HPDE).

Comments: Current work-flow and process management tools are not well integrated with the process and data modeling tools and component repositories used by IS organizations. Tool integration costs can be substantial.

Interestingly, this approach can also be an accelerator when applied to the requirements-discovery process for future state process design. Modeling work flows instead of process hierarchies seems to get a better answer faster.

Additional References: Work flow is a fashionable topic at the moment and there is a considerable literature, both theoretical and anecdotal, on its application to business process design. Less attention has been paid to the use of work flow principles in the design of IT processes.

Accelerator 9. Development on the Desktop for Groups

Description: Move development from mainframe-based shared services technologies to individual desktops and group local area network (LAN) platforms and provide group-oriented tools and processes for developers.

Used by: E&Y LLP
National City Bank
Sonoco
Xerox
Pacific Gas & Electric

Used for: Shift-development costs and performance from mainframe cycles to LAN/Desktop. Remove resource bottlenecks associated with mainframe-based development and time-sharing systems.

Expected Effects: Productivity improvement of 35–50 percent through better PC/LAN performance and reduced waiting times. Better and more functional tools available on local workstations and networks also improve individual and group performance. Reduced costs/seat for developers after the first year.

Observed Effects: Actual improvements of 20–40 percent in Design, Construction, & Test for some environments.

Combine with: HPDE. Support Infrastructure.

Comments: Many organizations based their original cost estimates on survey data from Gartner Group and others collected during the mid-1980s.[2] The data indicated that the cost of supporting a single developer on an IBM MVS-class host system was around $25,000 per year. The cost of providing a comparable set of workstation-based tools and technologies would be around $30,000 in the first year and perhaps $10,000 per year thereafter. It was expected, therefore, that significant cost savings would accrue after the first year.

In practice, the heavy support requirements of workstations and networks, the need to constantly update the capability of the workstations and networks used by developers, and the repeated release of new versions of the tools that they use has eroded this expected cost advantage. Mainframe "mips" have also become cheaper as application investment has shifted from the data center to a more distributed technological environment.

Our best data indicate that development on the desktop is only slightly cheaper over a five-year period than host-based development. There are also compatibility issues to consider, since few

[2] Based on material published by the Gartner Group in a series of research reports between 1988 and 1993.

desktop environments are exact analogs of the target implementation environment for the developments that they support. Nevertheless, despite the cost and compatibility concerns, productivity is still better than on traditional shared-resource host systems.

Where the available PC-based tools do not provide a close emulation of the target platform, productivity gains are significantly lower but still present. There are continuing issues of software configuration management and version control for LAN-based group environments. System integration is required to maintain an effective infrastructure—increasing the cost of the approach significantly.

Additional References

Leading Practices Report—1.1: A Summary of Leading Practices within the Systems Delivery Process. A report of a joint project of Ernst & Young and the Society for Information Management. (1993). Available from Ernst & Young LLP, Center for Business Innovation, One Walnut Street, Boston, MA 02108, or from local chapters of the Society for Information Management (SIM).

Accelerator 10. Management by Fact

Description: Introduce objective process measures and publish the results on a regular basis. Provide education in technological limitations and a realistic analysis of IT and IS capabilities to customers. Systematically monitor projects and analyze sources of variation. Implement a proactive process-improvement program based on the results.

Used by: Citizens' Coke & Gas
E&Y LLP
Springs Industries

Used for: Improve IS and project management's ability to control and modify projects and manage customer expectations.

Expected Effects: Better controls on progress of project. Better scope management. Better management of resources. Fewer unrealistic time tables or expectations from technology.

Observed Effects: Observed reduction in number of adjustments to estimate-to-complete (ETC) and estimate-at-completion (EAC) data during last third of a project. Improved initial prediction of the project delivery date. However, the total number of schedule and completion estimate adjustments remains about the same, or increases slightly.

Combine with: Move Work into Infrastructure. Process Measurement.

Comments: Focuses on the availability of more frequent and better focused management information. It is necessary, however, to take care with over-control/over-reaction issues that sometimes result from the availability of timely status information. IS organizations that adopt this accelerator are encouraged to develop an *annual fitness report* for the IS organization. Note that, as management by fact is implemented, project estimates do not necessarily get smaller—but the estimates are more realistic.

Additional References: Many of the issues associated with management by fact are project-management issues related to the behavioral traits of project managers and the cultures in which they are forced to operate. In the long term, the culture, not just the project management process, must change. See, for example:

Arthur, L. J. (1985). *Measuring Programmer Productivity and Software Quality.* New York: John Wiley & Sons.

Block, R. (1983). *The Politics of Projects.* Englewood Cliffs, NJ: Yourdon Press.

DeMarco, T., & Lister, T. (1987). *Peopleware: Productive Projects and Teams.* New York: Dorset House.

Gilb, T. (1977). *Software Metrics.* Winthrop Publishers.

Gilb, T. (1988). *Principles of Software Engineering Management.* New York: Addison-Wesley.

Glass, R. L. (1992). *Building Quality Software.* Englewood Cliffs, NJ: Prentice-Hall.

King, D. (1992). *Project Management Made Simple.* Englewood Cliffs, NJ: Yourdon Press.

Thomsett, R. (1993). *Third Wave Project Management.* Englewood Cliffs, NJ: Yourdon Press.

Accelerator 11. High-Performance Development Environment (HPDE) Technology for Work Groups and Mechanization of Work

Description: Develop, buy, build, and integrate sets of tools that mechanize appropriate parts of the development process. Implement tools on desktop/LAN platform and in support of the transition from the development environment to the implementation environment.

Used by: American Quarter Horse
Ameritech
Apple
Bally Corp.
Burlington Industries
Capital EMI Records
Canadian International Bank of Commerce
Citizens' Coke & Gas
Conoco
Dryfus
E&Y LLP
Farmers Insurance

First Direct Bank Ltd.
Imperial Oil
Long Island Lighting Co.
Owens Corning Fiberglass
Pacific Gas & Electric
Panhandle Eastern
Piedmont Natural Gas
R.J. Reynolds
SeaLand Containers Inc.
Severn-Trent Water Co.
Sonoco
USA Group
Wachovia Financial Services

Used for: Provide technology leverage through pre-integrated infrastructure components that support the software design-and-construction processes.

Expected Effects: Reduction in Design/Code/Test effort by at least 60 percent.

Observed Effects: Observed reductions of more than 75 percent in applications developed for character-based environments. Reduction of 40–50 percent in applications development for Graphical User Interface environments where consistent standards are developed and enforced by the HPDE tools.

Combine with: Development on the Desktop. JAD. Prototypes. Component Reuse. Support Infrastructure.

Comments: The HPDE approach works especially well for code generation and some aspects of testing. There is a high impact on a limited part of the overall software development life cycle. It is also possible to use hybrid strategies, such as the data warehouse principle, to attack large backlogs of "information delivery" and decision support requirements. The IS organization still needs to take care with overengineered solutions that no one wants to pay for. "Just because you *can* doesn't mean you *should*"—should be applied as a sanity check when building HPDE functionality. Too much technology can result in "confuse-a-user" situations where the business need is lost in "technobabble." In the early days of HPDE implementation, take care that the steep learning curve that may be required does not skew results. Also be prepared for continuing integration and maintenance requirements from the HPDE technologies themselves.

Additional References: There is a surprisingly limited literature on effective tool integration. I suspect this is so because few people have really solved the problem in a standard way. See, for example:

Boone, G. H., Merlyn, V. P., & Dobratz, R. E. (1990). *The 2nd Annual Report on CASE*. Bellevue, WA: CASE Research Corporation.

Brown, A. W., Carney, D. J., Morris, E. J., Smith, D. B., & Zarrella, P. F. (1994). *Principles of CASE Tool Integration*. New York: Oxford University Press.

Parkinson, J. (1991). *Making CASE Work*. Manchester, England: NCC Blackwell.

Accelerator 12. Provision of Examples/Model-Based Development/Use of Templates

Description: Find, develop, and use models and examples as starting points for development projects. Collect and display fully working models or real applications as a way to verify customer requirements. Predetermine the integration and implementation requirements of software, based on experience elsewhere.

Used by: Baxter Health Care
E&Y LLP
Gateway 2000

National City Bank
Nutrasweet

Used for: Accelerate discovery process using specification by example and provide design templates for solution deliverables.

Expected Effects: Reduce effort and cycle time by starting with most of the solution.

Observed Effects: A reduction of 50 to 75 percent in the resources and 70 to 80 percent in the elapsed time required for effective requirements analysis. A reduction of 35 to 40 percent in the resources required and 65 to 80 percent in the elapsed time for the Design/Code/Test process. A reduction in 75 to 90 percent in defects related to badly stated requirements and poor design specifications.

Combine with: JAD. Prototyping. Cross-Functional Teams. HPDE.

Comments: To be effective the examples used must be understandable in the context of the customer's process. Achieving savings in the Design/Code/Test process depends on the availability and use of effective version management and configuration control tools.

Accelerator 13. Groupware

Description: Introduce and deploy infrastructure and tools that support intra- and inter-group communication. Design and implement coordination processes that use these tools. Develop a program of incentives to reward collaborative behavior.

Used by: E&Y LLP
IBM

Used for: Improved intra-team communications and easier collaborative working. Reduced process defects resulting from poor communications and coordination failures. Accelerate the deployment of best practices. Foster the development of a knowledge-enabled organization.

Expected Effects: Reduce the administrative proportion of project overhead by 50 percent through more timely and effective communication. Decreased process variability and increased use of selected practices. Reduced related to incorrect use of the preferred process.

Observed Effects: Reduction of 35 to 70 percent in project administration overhead. Better project-management records and audit trails. Rapid rise in the contribution of "help and hints" material, even without incentives.

Combine with: HPDE. Migrate Work into Infrastructure. Reward-and-Recognition Programs.

Comments: To a large extent, the initial effectiveness depends on the sophistication and extent of available infrastructure. Almost universal coverage needs to be achieved as fast as possible. In situations where the deployment of these facilities is rapid and extensive, major improvements can be achieved with little or no additional effort. The IS staff will adopt the technology and use it, because it is to their benefit to do so. A well-designed reward-and-recognition program for both contributors and users will help to sustain the initial momentum.

Additional References

Tannenbaum, A. (1994). Workgroup Repositories to Developer Desktops. *Application Development Trends, 1(4).*

Accelerator 14. Performance Support Systems

Description: Provide immediate access to reference and support materials that are relevant to the work of individual developers and project teams. Ensure that no one is more than a few seconds away from required reference materials, process guidelines, or problem-resolution assistance.

Used by: Apple
E&Y LLP
Farmers Insurance
IBM
Microsoft

Used for: Reduce the learning time for staff working in new or unfamiliar environments. Reduce or eliminate process failures related to limited competencies and lack of experience. Promote the deployment and consistent use of best practices. Eliminate the creation and dissemination of individual's solutions to common problems when a better solution is known. Encourage the use of common reference knowledge and common practices.

Expected Effects: Dramatic reduction in self-created process variations related to a lack of understanding of the standard process. Reduction in the time spent solving commonly occurring problems, a performance support system can reduce the time spent solving such common problems by 75 to 85 percent and improve the quality of the solution that is adopted by presenting the preferred answer immediately.

Combine with: Coaching by Experts. Groupware.

Comments: Once again, the initial effectiveness depends on the sophistication and extent of the infrastructure available to support performance support tools and processes. If, in addition to routine help and guidelines, access is made available to the experience and advice of process and technology experts, either directly or through a knowledge base search facility, even complex problems can be resolved quickly and effectively.

Our research on performance support uncovered an unexpected and, so far, unexplained phenomenon. If performance support was not available, staff faced with a problem could usually (in excess of

95 percent of the situations we saw) work out an answer, although it could take them from minutes to days to do so. This answer was only as good or better than the available best practice in about 15 percent of cases. In the remainder, the answer was less effective, although it did usually work. The surprising effect was, however, related to the relative extent of propagation of the solutions. Answers that were worse than the known best practice spread to many more people, and much faster, than did the good or better answers. Thus, more and more staff came into contact with less than the best available practices if performance support was not in place. We have not attempted to measure the productivity and effectiveness reduction that this observation implies, but it may well be substantial.

Accelerator 15. Heterogeneous Component Strategies

Description: Assume that there is "no single right answer" to all business problems. Match the technology used in the solution to the requirements of the problem. Do not try to solve everything with the same set of technologies.

Used by: E&Y LLP
Barclays Bank
LTV Steel

Used for: Reduce the effort required to fit in an inappropriate solution technology to the needs of the business problem.

Expected Effects: Reduce or eliminate the effort required to modify a standard technology so that it is optimized to the specific needs of a business process. Improved customer satisfaction and better realization of benefits through the development of better-targeted solutions.

Observed Effects: The required modification effort is indeed reduced, sometimes by as much as 15 to 20 percent of the overall project resource requirement. However, systems integration issues, represented by the effort required to integrate a new set of technologies with the current infrastructure, often predominate in observed results. Net gains are usually modest, unless the standard technology would be a very bad mismatch to the business need.

Combine with: Buy or Assemble vs. Rebuild. Economies-of-Scope.

Comments: There is a trade-off here between the simplicity of supporting a single solution (and the associated reduced technology integration effort) and the benefit that accrues from a specific solution. When economies-of-scope and demand-management considerations are added, this accelerator requires judicious use to deliver the potential benefits.

Accelerator 16. Re-engineering of Legacy Data

Description: Capture the essential business value represented by legacy systems using portfolio analysis tools and the extraction of metadata definitions. Use re-engineering tools and processes to move data structures from current- to future-state platforms. Derive maintainable data models from physical file and database designs.

Used by: Ameritech
Banco de Portugal
Capitol EMI Records
E&Y LLP
GTE Telephone Operations
Hewlett Packard
MBNA/SSBA
Norwich Union Assurance Group

Reynolds Metals
Scottish Widows Life Assurance Company
Sprint
Standard Life Assurancy Company
USAA
Wheeling Pittsburgh Steel Co.

Used for: Reduce the cycle time required for application right sizing or platform conversion. Clean up data content prior to re-architecting applications in support of business process redesign. Reduce the cost of maintaining reference data sets by standardizing data values and definitions. Improve the maintainability of legacy applications by better documentation and rationalization of data definitions across applications.

Expected Effects: Reduce by half the effort required to maintain reference data that is used by multiple applications. Simplify the requirements for data management and database administration. Create platform-conversion possibilities for large legacy applications and data sets that would otherwise be too complex or expensive to undertake.

Observed Effects: Reductions of 50 to 70 percent in the estimated resource requirements for large-scale platform conversions or application redevelopment projects. Reductions in 20 to 75 percent in the effort required to maintain standard reference data sets and codes. Improved data documentation also has a productivity impact in both application-enhancement projects and new development projects that require access to legacy data.

Combine with: HPDE and Mechanization of Work.

Comments: The results that can be achieved depend a lot on both the source technology and (for platform conversions) the target platform. There have been more failures than successes over the past decade, but this is changing as the available support technology improves and our understanding of effective technology and data-reengineering processes grows. In situations where data are shared between many applications, data rationalization can be worthwhile in itself—even though the initial investment is almost always high. The best long-term results come when re-engineered data definitions are loaded into modeling tools for subsequent reuse.

Additional References

Goldberg, B., and Sifonis, J. G. (1995). Leveraging your Legacy Systems. *Data Management Review, 5(1).*

Hayes, I. S. (1994). Redevelopment Workbenches Free Programmers. *Application Development Trends, 1(3).*

Hayes, I. S. (1994). Protect Software Assets by Migrating Legacies. *Application Development Trends, 1(9).*

Hickey, G. L., & Jennings, R. A. (1994). USAA's Reengineering Turns IE on Its Head. *Application Development Trends, 1(2).*

Schmidt, J. (1994). Migration Strategy Follows from Database Type. *Application Development Trends, 1(7).*

Varriccho, J. (1994). Equitable Reengineers Years of Insurance Legacy Information. *Application Development Trends, 1(9).*

Accelerator 17. Development of 80/20 Solutions and Requirements Evolution

Description: Make extensive use of application prototyping to build functioning and implementable prototypes. The focus of this accelerator is on building the essential minimum of required business support functionality as quickly as possible, and implementing this partial solution before adding new functions or improving the initially delivered capabilities.

Used by: Ameritech
Citizens' Coke & Gas
Eastman Kodak

E&Y LLP
First Union Bank
R.J. Reynolds
Springs Industries
Xerox

Used for: Reduce the cycle time required to develop the initial version of an application. Get new process support essentials working as fast as possible. Reduce the level of rework that stems from poorly defined or "blue-sky" requirements that remain unchallenged until implementation.

Expected Effects: Reduce the time to deliver an initial version of an application by at least 75 percent. Reduce the defects related to poor requirements definition by 75 percent. Reduce the time to initial implementation by 80 percent.

Observed Effects: There is an observed average reduction of 50 to 75 percent in the initial time to deliver. The initial application versions tend to represent 30 to 40 percent of the expected "final" business support requirements.

Combine with: HPDE. Reuse. JAD. Cross-Functional Teams.

Comments: The results that can be achieved depend on the nature of the business requirement, the application being developed, and the degree of integration with current applications and technology that is required.

Accelerator 18. Buy or Assemble vs. Build

Description: Try to buy a complete solution or assemble the solution from bought-in components rather than custom-develop the components or the complete application.

Used by: Amgen
Black & Decker
BP Oil Europe
Citizens' Coke & Gas
CompUSA
E&Y LLP
Hewlett Packard
IBM
Mattel
Owens Corning Fiberglass
Sabre Travel Information Network
TRW
Xerox

Used for: Reduce the cycle time and the development cost for application and infrastructure development of complete business solutions.

Expected Effects: Reduction of 20 to 25 percent in development-and-delivery effort. Reduction of 70 percent in development cycle time.

Observed Effects: Results vary according to the effectiveness of the application or component-selection strategy and the degree of customization that is attempted. The best case seems to deliver about a 70 percent reduction in elapsed time. In some cases, the delivery process took longer than the estimates put forward for custom development.

Combine with: Reuse. HPDE. Cross-Functional Teams. 80/20 Solutions.

Comments: There is still a tendency to over-customize the purchased solution. PC-based single-user packages can be dramatically more cost-effective, but, even with these, there are data-integration issues with existing systems. Estimates often ignore the effort required to adapt business processes for use with the purchased software.

Accelerator 19. Sponsorship Education

Description: Ensure that the business executives who take on sponsor roles and responsibilities understand the commitments that are required. Provide proactive support for the desired sponsor behaviors.

Used by: Chemical Bank
E&Y LLP
South Carolina Electric & Gas

Used for: Create effective sustainable sponsorship. Avoid process failures resulting from lack of commitment after the initial agreement to a development project.

Expected Effects: Eliminate otherwise avoidable sponsor defections, or the removal or loss of continuing sponsorship. Eliminate projects that lose sponsorship during the project. Reduce the number of delays resulting from issue-resolution failures related to lack of available sponsorship.

Observed Effects: Exogenous factors still dominate sponsor-related behavior, although shorter projects tend to have fewer sponsor changes. Where sponsors do not change during a project, proactive sponsor education and support does reduce divisive or delaying issues. A sponsor change is often equivalent to rejustification of the project and almost always results in a delay, which is better experienced as early as possible after the change.

Combine with: Cross-Functional Teams. Management by Fact.

Comments: This is more of a disaster-avoidance strategy, based on the small number of results that we have collected so far.

Additional References: The Organizational Change Management literature is a rich source of guidance on sponsor management topics. See, for example:

Connor, D. R. (1993). *Managing at the Speed of Change: How Resilient Managers Succeed and Prosper when Others Fail.* New York: Villard Books.

Lewin, K. (1952). Group Decision and Social Change. In G. E. Swanson, T. N. Newcomb, & E. L. Hartley (Eds.), *Readings in Social Psychology* (Rev. Ed.). New York: Holt.

Schein. E. H. (1988). *Planning and Managing Change, Management in the 1990s.* Cambridge, MA: MIT Press.

Senge, P. M. (1990). *The Fifth Discipline: The Art and Practice of the Learning Organization.* New York: Doubleday.

Accelerator 20. Use the "Many Successful Projects" Approach

Description: Try to arrange for development to be organized as programs of small projects that can be managed successfully and deliver results quickly, rather than have huge and difficult-to-manage projects that take months or years to show a return.

Used by: AT&T
E&Y LLP
Society Corp.

Used for: Gain success in multiple small increments that can be effectively and successfully managed—not in a single large effort that is difficult to manage or cannot be managed successfully at all.

Expected Effects: Earlier delivery of business benefits results in easier justification for later projects. There should be fewer failures in delivery, and any failures that do occur should be small and easy to rectify. There should be reduced levels of rework.

Observed Effects: There are significant initial improvements in benefit delivery, quality, and cycle time from the early projects, but these are harder than expected to deploy to a large number of people working in the necessarily complex multi-project programs that result from this accelerator.

Combine with: JAD. Prototyping. Cross-Functional Teams. 80/20 Solutions.

Comments: Programs that consist of many tactical projects may have quality and effectiveness issues within the context of a strategic framework if the strategic perspective is not enforced within each project. There will be considerable strain put on the program managers to maintain the strategic focus and on knowledge coordination, to ensure that all participants in multi-project programs are kept in touch with progress.

Accelerator 21. Use of Multi-Functional Teams

Description: Encourage or require the participation of all impacted constituencies as members of the development team.

Used by: Ameritech
AT&T
Burlington Industries
Citizens' Coke & Gas
Coca-Cola Consolidated
E&Y LLP
First Union Bank
R.J. Reynolds
Sara Lee Hosiery
South Carolina Electric & Gas
Springs Industries
Wachovia Financial Services
Xerox

Used for: Involve all interested or impacted constituencies in problem definition and solution selection. Accelerate consensus on essentials and develop all aspects of solution in parallel. Reduce development effort and avoid rework. Shorten implementation time.

Expected Effects: Reduction in rework through a better requirements-definition process and more comprehensive customer participation in solution design. Reduction in cycle time through efficient issue resolution.

Observed Effects: Initially, the use of multi-function teams can actually slow down the development process, as team members learn to work together and develop effective operating practices. There is also a tendency to try to create a larger scope for the work as every team member attempts to have all of their perspectives included. If the initial process is effectively facilitated, subsequent gains can be significant, both in the quality of the initial solution and the reduction in the elapsed time required to achieve it.

Combine with: JAD. Prototyping. HPDE.

Comments: Geography can make this a difficult or expensive approach. Significant costs can be incurred when staff have to travel long distances to meetings and work away from their normal locations for several weeks. Extended absence for their normal role can also reduce the effectiveness of team members as spokespeople for the proposed solution.

We have seen the recent introduction of video teleconferencing technology as an attempt to create "virtual meetings," in which the participants do not have to travel to a common location to meet. Results appear to have been very mixed, with both significant successes and spectacular failures reported. We believe that VTC technology will have an increasingly important role to play in this area, but that it is, as yet, too expensive and not functional enough to be used on any but an experimental basis. Best results are obtained when the equipment is sophisticated, participants already know each other, and the absolute range of time shift required is not greater than four hours.

Accelerator 22. Strategic Alignment with the Business

Description: Work to ensure that all projects have value that contributes to the stated goals and objectives of the business. Adjust IS priorities as business priorities change.

Used by: Coca-Cola Consolidated
Eastman Kodak
E&Y LLP
IBM
Sara Lee Hosiery
South Carolina Electric & Gas
Springs Industries
Xerox

Used for: Build more of the right systems, targeted at priority needs set by the customer. Develop an ability to describe benefits in terms of measures used by the business.

Expected Effects: Get more synergy from supporting high-priority business needs. Create an ability to link delivered benefits to the strategic measures of the business. Eliminate projects for which there is no business sponsor. Create a culture in which some (small) proportion of projects are canceled before completion (because of changing business needs) and this is seen as a positive capability.

Observed Effects: IS organizations have a long way to go to fully implement this accelerator. Where progress has been most effective has been in developing effective dialogs with business executives, so that there are fewer "surprises" for the IS organization hidden in business plans. The development of effective ways to measure and report the value delivered from information systems remains a major hurdle.

Combine with: Management by Fact. Sponsor Education. Process Measurement.

Comments: Considering that this has been among IS executives' top ten concerns for about a decade now, it remains surprising that so little progress has been made in forging closer links between IS planning and business strategy.[3] As the need for infrastructure investment grows and the planning horizon of companies shortens, effective collaboration between the two planning functions gets more critical. Companies who have figured this out are markedly more effective users of Information Technology than those who have not.

Additional References: Although strategic alignment has been a topic of interest for IS organizations for many years, it has remained an elusive goal. There is, however, an extensive literature on available approaches, from Critical Success Factor Analysis to Sociotechnical Systems Analysis. See, for example:

Eliot, L. B. (1994). Aligning Business Goals to Software Development. *Application Development Trends, 1*(2).

Goldberg, B., & Sifonis, J. G. (1994). *Dynamic Planning: The Art of Managing Beyond Tomorrow*. New York: Oxford University Press.

Keen, P. G. W. (1991). *Shaping the Future: Business Design through Information Technology*. Boston: Harvard Business School Press.

[3]Annual surveys of the top ten concerns of CIOs and their executive equivalents are available from a variety of sources, including Index Group (now part of Computer Sciences Corporation), the Center for Studies in Data Processing (CSDP) at George Washington University, and the Center for Information Systems Research (CISR) at MIT. The actual concerns vary from year to year, but have shown a steady transition away from pure technology issues and toward the need to support strategic alignment and the demonstration of business value.

"Leading Practices Report—1.1. A Summary of Leading Practices within the Systems Delivery Process." (Report of a joint project of Ernst & Young and the Society for Information Management.) (1993). Available from Ernst & Young LLP, Center for Business Innovation, One Walnut Street, Boston MA, 02108, or from SIM.

McGee, J. V. (1992). *What Is Strategic Performance Measurement? (Ernst and Young LLP Center for Business Innovation. Research Note)*, March.

Prusak, L., & McGee, J. V. (1993). *Managing Information Strategically*. New York: John Wiley & Sons.

Venkatraman, N. (1991). IT-Induced Business Reconfiguration. In M. S. Scott Morton (Ed.), *The Corporation of the 1990's: Information Technology and Organizational Transformation*. New York: Oxford University Press.

Accelerator 23. Process Measurement

Description: Ensure that there is an effective process-measurement program and that the results are used to drive improvements efforts.

Used by: E&Y LLP
IBM
Sara Lee Hosiery
Society Corp.
Springs Industries

Used for: Identify high-priority areas for process improvement and focus efforts on high payback opportunities. Support an improved recognition-and-reward process for teams and (eventually) individuals.

Expected Effects: Reduce the amount of unplanned work. Identify and eliminate as many sources of inefficiency as possible. Provide better practitioner support in complex, difficult, or weak areas of the development process.

Observed Effects: There is an initial 10 to 15 percent "spurt" in productivity as the measurement program is deployed, mostly due to the Hawthorne effect.[4] This is difficult to sustain, unless improvement targets are quickly identified and the necessary process changes addressed.

Combine with: Management by Fact. Performance Support Systems.

Comments: Introducing an effective measurement program is not easy to do. Nor is it easy to calibrate or interpret early results. Care has to be taken to avoid misuse of the data from the initial measurement process. Effective targeting for early improvements is also critical to establish the value of quantitative and objective performance data.

Additional References: There is a fairly good literature on the need for and effect of measurement programs in IS organizations. In fact, it sometimes seems to me that there is more written about measurement than there are measurement programs. Nevertheless, Grady's two books on the long-term IS development metrics program at Hewlett Packard provide an excellent source of comparative cost information for measurement efforts.

[4]This refers to the work of Elton Mayo, an industrial psychologist, which led to a series of experiments, called the Hawthorne Experiments, conducted at Western Electric's Hawthorne Facility. Although these experiments led to significant findings in terms of principles of individual and group involvement in quality programs, they are most famous for one finding—the so-called *Hawthorne Effect*. This came from one experiment where productivity was observed to increase when the lighting level was increased. When the level was then lowered, to the researchers' surprise, the productivity again increased. The ultimate interpretation is that people perform better when they are the focus of attention, and when they try something new.

Current Practices in Measuring Quality. (1989). The Conference Board, Inc., Research Bulletin No. 234. New York: Author.

Eccles, R. G. (1991). The Performance Measurement Manifesto. *Harvard Business Review, 69(1).*

Johnson, J. (1994). How We Climbed to Maturity Level Two. *Application Development Trends, 1(4).*

Grady, R. B. (1992). *Practical Software Metrics for Project Management.* Englewood Cliffs, NJ: Prentice-Hall.

Grady, R. B., & Casewell, D. L. (1987). *Software Metrics: Establishing a Company-wide Program.* Englewood Cliffs, NJ: Prentice-Hall.

Kaplan, R. S., & Norton, D. P. (1992). The Balanced Scorecard—Measures That Drive Performance. *Harvard Business Review, 70(1).*

Rubin, H. A. (1995). Measurement: Despite Promise, Successful Programs Rare. *Application Development Trends, 2(1).*

Accelerator 24. Copy Leading Practices from External Sources

Description: Identify the source and understand the effect of leading practices in other organizations. Identify practices that will be effective in your organization and culture. Introduce appropriate practices and measure their effect.

Used by: Apple
Eastman Kodak
E&Y LLP
IBM
McDonald's
Xerox

Used for: Jump-start the process-improvement initiative by focusing on existing practices in similar organizations who have already made similar improvements to those desired. Adopt those that match the local IS situation.

Expected Effects: Identify and deploy a higher proportion of successful practices than would result from internally focused improvement efforts.

Observed Effects: The best source of practices seems to be companies that are similar or a little ahead of yours. The best ideas do not necessarily come from companies in the same market. Looking outside can provide fresh insights that would not necessarily be discovered by the companies within an existing market, no matter how good a source of best practices they might otherwise be.

Combine with: Strategic Alignment. Management by Fact. Process Measurement.

Comments: Not the same as benchmarking, but benchmarking is often a key component of the process of identifying and implementing the leading practices of others. Note that the General Electric benchmark for continuous improvement is between 6 and 9 percent per year productivity gain. Leading practices research and selection can push this into the 20 percent to 25 percent per year range for a while, but, as you get better, improvements get harder to achieve.

Additional References: There is an extensive literature on benchmarking and on the dangers of the careless adoption and use of the leading practices of others. See, for example:

Camp, R. C. (1989). *Benchmarking: The Search for Industry Best Practices That Lead to Superior Performance*. Milwaukee: Quality Press/American Society for Quality Control.

Kash, D. E. (1989). *Perpetual Innovation: The New World of Competition*. New York: Basic Books.

Peters, T. (1994). *The Tom Peters Seminar: Crazy Times Call for Crazy Organizations*. New York: Random House.

Schwartz, P. (1991). *The Art of the Long View*. New York: Doubleday.
Watson, G. H. (1993). *Strategic Benchmarking*. New York: John Wiley & Sons.

Mapping the Acceleration Practices to the Five Groups of Approaches

Table 7.1 maps the 24 practices described above to the five groups of acceleration strategies.

Table 7.1 *Acceleration—Mapping Practices to Strategies*

Practice	Management of Demand	Elimination of Work	Elimination of Rework	Parallel Working	Provision of Tools
1. Migrate work into infrastructure		xxxxxx		xxxxxx	xxxxxx
2. Work elimination through process specialization		xxxxxx	xxxxxx		
3. Self-managed teams			xxxxxx	xxxxxx	
4. Reuse, using the "Builders & Buyers" model		xxxxxx	xxxxxx	xxxxxx	xxxxxx

(Table continues on next page)

Table 7.1 *(Continued)*

Practice	Management of Demand	Elimination of Work	Elimination of Rework	Parallel Working	Provision of Tools
5. Coaching by experts			xxxxxx		
6. Economics of scope	xxxxxx	xxxxxx	xxxxxx		xxxxxx
7. High participation intensity discovery processes		xxxxxx	xxxxxx	xxxxxx	
8. Work-flow management		xxxxxx		xxxxxx	xxxxxx
9. Development on the desktop				xxxxxx	xxxxxx
10. Management by fact	xxxxxx				
11. Mechanization of work				xxxxxx	xxxxxx
12. Provision of examples	xxxxxx	xxxxxx	xxxxxx	xxxxxx	xxxxxx
13. Groupware			xxxxxx	xxxxxx	xxxxxx
14. Performance support systems			xxxxxx	xxxxxx	xxxxxx
15. Heterogeneous component strategies					xxxxxx
16. Re-engineering of legacy data		xxxxxx	xxxxxx		xxxxxx
17. 80/20 solutions		xxxxxx	xxxxxx	xxxxxx	xxxxxx

Table 7.1 *(Continued)*

Practice	Management of Demand	Elimination of Work	Elimination of Rework	Parallel Working	Provision of Tools
18. Buy or assemble vs. build	xxxxxx	xxxxxx	xxxxxx		
19. Sponsorship education	xxxxxx		xxxxxx		
20. "Many successful projects"	xxxxxx		xxxxxx	xxxxxx	
21. Multi-functional teams		xxxxxx	xxxxxx	xxxxxx	
22. Strategic alignment with the business	xxxxxx	xxxxxx			
23. Process measurement		xxxxxx	xxxxxx	xxxxxx	xxxxxx
24. Copy leading practices	xxxxxx	xxxxxx	xxxxxx		xxxxxx

8

Catalog of Deceleration Practices

In this kind of a war, I *only have to get it right* once *to beat you.* You *people have to get it right* every time *just to avoid losing. Who would you bet on?*

—Attributed to MAO TSE TUNG

Decelerators and How to Avoid Them

What Is a Decelerator?

In our research, a *decelerator* was any commonly observed practice that consistently *increased* the cycle time of any process of which it was a part, or to which it was applied. We looked for practices that were observable in more than one organization, to reduce the degree of organizational and cultural bias in the results (although we acknowledge that some bias remains). We also looked for practices that were repeatedly used or that were encountered by the same or different teams in multiple organizations, reducing the bias that results from only considering "pathological" process problems or from the presence of the "F-team" effect.[1]

Provenance and Cautions

Although our data on decelerators come from essentially the same sources as those for the acceleration practices described in Chapter 7, all of the cautions provided up to now apply with *twice* the emphasis to this chapter. Few of the organizations we worked with would like to own up publicly to the idea that they were actively subverting, in some sense, their own improvement efforts. Yet virtually all were doing so to some extent, some of the time. We

[1]Here we use the term "F-team" to describe the all too common results of our least capable employees migrating to the "bottom" of the resource pool, from where they occasionally (and, despite our best efforts) get assigned as a group to a critical project.

were able to do much less quantitative analysis of these practices, and the results we saw are arguable in detail, if true in general. Nor did we get the chance to try out many of the avoidance strategies that the research participants suggested.

In many ways, this is a supreme irony for those searching for performance improvement. In most intsances, substantial gains can be had simply by *stopping* the practices described in this section—usually without expending any real effort or requiring a significant resource investment. The potential gains are large and low cost. The changes required are usually small and the rewards great. Why then is it so difficult to remove the plethora of decelerators that we found?

Because removing them means giving up on cherished beliefs and behaviors, many of which stand right at the heart of the IS organization's culture and identity. It means modifying behaviors and habits that were seen as successful in the past. It often means taking risks, without the certainty of reward in a culture that has become rather risk-averse. In short, it means change at a very personal level. Thus it is a difficult and dangerous process.

Decelerator 1. Fear of Failure or Litigation

Description: This is a common cultural factor where it is believed that no project can be allowed to fail. As a result, few risks are taken to adopt new or improved processes. Fear of litigation, in circumstances where the system will support a key business area with serious consequences of failure, can also be a factor here.

Identified by: E&Y LLP
Eli Lilly

We also collected a good deal of unstructured anecdotal material from the pharmaceutical, financial services, and utility companies with whom we worked.

Observed Effects: The most obvious effect is an unwillingness to experiment or take risks. This will often translate into a rhetoric of "we must do leading-edge projects, but only when the technology is proven." Actual development activity will be slow, very conventional in process, and relatively unchanged over time. There may also be higher than average staff turnover if younger IS personnel perceive that their skills are falling behind the market, and/or an older than average group of IS staff who have "retired" in place to take advantage of an unchanging IS environment with which they are familiar.

Address with: Strategic benchmarking and the careful identification of practices that can be introduced with low visible risk but that have high impact. Consider outsourcing only as a last resort, since this would be outsourcing the problem—which is rarely successful.

Comments: A very difficult situation to change quickly, especially if it has persisted for some time. If the principal point of resistance is the CIO or an equivalent executive, it may be necessary to focus education and awareness building before attempting to introduce new practices.

Additional References

Zells, L. (1994). Litigated Disaster: Anatomy of a Major Project Failure. *Application Development Trends, 1*(*12*).

Decelerator 2. Complexity of Business Process to Legacy System Associations

Description: It may be too difficult to disentangle current systems and processes, or the smallest available set of viable impacts may be too large to handle in one project.

Identified by: Boeing
Capitol EMI
E&Y LLP
Farmers Insurance
Hewlett Packard

Observed Effects: Over time, the interaction between business processes and the systems that support them can become complex and may not be well understood. If these associations are too complex, any attempt to replace a small part of the information systems portfolio will require extensive interfacing to integrate the new applications with the remaining parts of the original systems or processes. The effort required to implement and operate these interfaces can overwhelm the actual development effort and, in extreme cases, a stable result may be technically or economically impossible. This tends to cause a paralysis based on the huge size of any viable project.

Address with: Portfolio analysis and data re-engineering can begin to disentangle the legacy systems portfolio and simplify application interfaces. Combined with limited process-redesign efforts, there is usually potential to find areas where small or medium-sized improvement projects can be chartered at acceptable levels of risk.

Where large complex areas of association remain, consider the wholesale replacement of legacy systems by purchased software packages.

Comments: This is a very common problem and is a real barrier to getting started. In many cases, preliminary portfolio analysis will show avenues of attack that are not obvious from casual observation. It is common for the majority of the maintenance workload to originate from a small proportion of heavily interconnected applications and data sets. Addressing these first can result in a major efficiency boost and improved customer service.

Decelerator 3. Destabilized IS Processes

Description: The current state of the IS organization's development-and-delivery processes may be in such a mess that it cannot be repaired within acceptable parameters.

Identified by: E&Y LLP

Observed Effects: The Software Engineering Institute's Capability Maturity Model (CMM) (see Additional References) for software processes defines the lowest level as "Chaotic" with no common or repeatable processes, no process measurement, and poor or inconsistent process management. Most IS organizations (probably 80 percent of the total population by SEI estimates) are at this level. The remainder are mostly at Level 2, with a very few at Level 3 or 4. As of the start of 1995, only one IS group had been certified at Level 5, with another group believed to be there but as yet uncertified.[2,3] The CMM comes with an assessment process designed to help organizations move from the Chaotic level to progressively more effective practices and successive levels (repeatable, measured, managed, optimized).

It has always been assumed that Level 1 was as bad as it gets as far as process maturity is concerned. Our observations lead us to offer a slightly different viewpoint.

We believe that there are two additional Levels below Chaotic on the SEI scale. We call these Levels *Unconscious incompetence* or Level −1, and *Conscious incompetence* or Level −2.

An IS organization exhibits unconscious incompetence when its management practices tend to result in the wrong process being

[2] IBM's Space Systems Group, then part of the Federal Systems Division, since sold.

[3] Motorola Inc.'s software development operation, based in Bangalore, India.

chosen for most types of projects. These organizations appear chaotic, because they seldom repeat the processes they use, but this lack of repeatability is a direct consequence of process failures caused by bad process choices. Unconsciously incompetent organizations usually *think* that they are at Level 2, but can't understand why they always fail the assessment. We classify them as *unconsciously* incompetent, because their managers don't realize that it is their own management practices that are largely at fault.

Consciously incompetent IS organizations, on the other hand, *do* know that it is their management practices that are at the root of their problems, but they *consciously refuse* to do anything about it.

Of the 80 percent of organizations who would previously be classified as Level 1, we estimate that about 15 percent should be at Level −2 and about 50 percent at Level −1. The remaining 15 percent are actually simple chaotic. This analysis explains, in part, why so few IS organizations seem able to make it out of Level 1. Most of them aren't in Level 1 yet.

Address with: Awareness-building and sponsor education; benchmarking and comparative assessment (the SEI approach is a good place to start); and examples of best practices. Measurement programs also work well, but are difficult to start, because they will be actively resisted in almost all minus-one and minus-two situations.

Comments: If being at Level 1 is equivalent to the phrase "When you are up to your neck in alligators, it's hard to remember that it's your job to drain the swamp," then Level −1 is equivalent to not knowing what an alligator is, and Level −2 is equivalent to being in the alligator-breeding business.

Additional References

Paulk, M. C. et al. (1991). *Capability Maturity Model for Software.* Pittsburgh: Software Engineering Institute, Carnegie Mellon University.

Decelerator 4. Hostile or Ambivalent Project Teams

Description: Just because you have a better way to work doesn't mean everyone else will want to work your way. Project teams that have their own approach may not want to give it up, especially if it has been reasonably successful in the past. Without active participation in the new approaches, the status quo will quickly reassert itself and any short-term gains will be lost.

Identified by: Citizens' Coke & Gas
E&Y LLP

Observed Effects: There may be overt resistance ("We have no intention of doing it this way," or "Our project type isn't suitable") to the new approaches, practices, and tools, or, worse, covert opposition ("Sure, we'll give it a try"—but no one actually does so).

Address with: Awareness-building. Sponsor education. Focus on those individuals who are seen as sources of influence by their peers and try to recruit them to the new approach. Create recognition-and-reward programs that provide incentive for the new behavior and publicize the early successes. Make sure you have early successes to publicize.

Comments: Overt resistance can be managed, although it takes a large amount of change agent time and effective sponsorship to do so. It's much more difficult to deal with covert resistance.

Decelerator 5. Inflexibility of the Development Process

Description: Failure to recognize that all customers are not the same and that the IS development-and-delivery process must be adjusted to their needs, understanding, and capabilities.

Identified by: AT&T
Citizens' Coke & Gas

Observed Effects: There are many process failures because the development process used is not sufficiently specialized to the needs of the customer. Attempts to speed-up development and delivery result in high defect rates, because no one knows exactly how to modify the standard process to improve delivery. There is low customer satisfaction with the IS organization and many customers are looking elsewhere for IT solutions.

Address with: Adopt one of the available customizable process approaches and tool sets. Education project managers in better project structuring and planning. Focus on early process improvements and improved customer satisfaction.

Comments: This is probably the easiest decelerator to deal with, in the sense that a solution is readily available. Nevertheless, the solution is often rejected as too expensive or difficult to implement.

Decelerator 6. The IS Organization Does Not Have a Clear Vision of Its Relationship with Its Customers

Description: If the IT organization cannot articulate its vision of partnership it will not be able to implement it. In many instances this comes down to a mismatch between the strategic identity choice of the IS organization, and the desires of its customers.

Identified by: BP Exploration
E&Y LLP

Observed Effects: The IS organization pursues an internally consistent set of improvement objectives, but these do not match the business's idea of what the ideal IS organization should be like. There is growing frustration on both sides, because the improvement efforts that everyone in IS is making, often at considerable personal cost, never do seem to satisfy the customers. Eventually, either someone notices the problem (it usually takes an outsider to do this), or the IS improvement effort burns out.

Address with: Strategic Identity awareness-building. Sponsor education. IS management education.

Comments: This is an insidious problem indeed, especially when there is no easy way to communicate the lack of alignment between what IS wants to be and what the business wants them to be. The situation is further complicated by the inevitable plurality of customer demand for the IS organization's most effective identity.

Decelerator 7. JAD Process Failures

Description: JAD processes are used, but the teams are too small, facilitators are inadequately experienced, or team members lack credibility with customers. Workshop schedules are inflexible and do not match the needs of the project nor the workshop participants. Work products are of poor quality and are not delivered on time.

Identified by: Citizens' Coke & Gas
E&Y LLP

Observed Effects: If workshop-based, requirements-discovery and -solution design processes fail, they normally do so in a fairly spectacular way, leaving no easy way to recover. Once a workshop has failed it is normally necessary to fall back on more traditional process for requirements discovery and solution acceptance. This takes time and requires careful handling to limit the negative effects of the workshop failure.

Address with: Facilitator training and careful selection of workshop participants. Sponsor education to ensure that the necessary participants are made available and that business units know why they should make the appropriate people available for extended periods. Better initial briefing of new participants, so that expectations are correctly set, is also necessary.

Comments: Although facilitation training makes everyone better able to participate in a facilitated workshop, it seems that facilitators are born rather than made. Their skills can be improved through training and coaching, but facilitation requires attitudes and behaviors that cannot really be taught to those who are not already predisposed to them. If there are too few capable facilitation resources available, the workshop process will fail.

Decelerator 8. Lack of Access to Subject Matter Experts

Description: In some areas, access to subject matter experts, or, at the very least, access to their knowledge, is essential. If you don't have enough timely access, process failures or project delays will result. In some critical business and technology areas, lack of expert review at key milestones can result in the creation of a solution that cannot be implemented, but this will not be apparent until implementation is attempted.

Identified by: Citizens' Coke & Gas
E&Y LLP

Observed Effects: Requirements are generally unreasonable or poorly prioritized. There is no linkage to business priorities and essential business support functionality may be missing from the requirements. Current issues will tend to dominate articulated requirements at the expense of strategic business concerns. Solutions are "feature rich but function poor," and may require much more technology than planned to implement them. Some solutions may be impossible to implement using available technology or resources.

Address with: Sponsor education, to show the need for external input and review. Improved peer review processes within the IS organization and the business. Where internal expertise is not available, negotiate better access to business and technology subject matter experts at the start of the project, going outside the IS organization if necessary.

Comments: The most extreme case we have ever seen of this problem was at a pharmaceutical company, where a new worldwide inventory management system had been specified and developed. The system used Digital Equipment Corporation's *VAX* series of computers and a distributed relational database. It would have linked the manufacturing, warehousing, distribution, and wholesale distributors into one single, real-time inventory. The inventory managers would know, virtually to the minute, where everything within their inventory was, when it would be delivered, or available for delivery, and what it was costing them to deliver. Eventually, the system would extend to hospitals, physicians' offices, and retail pharmacies. It was truly a state-of-the-art solution to an inventory-management and product-shelf-life-management problem.

The IS organization had never worked with *VAX* computers before and were new to the issues of relational database design. They decided not to use DEC's own relational database and to go with a brand new version of a market leading product that had just been enhanced to support distributed data management. The project team was about 75 people, of whom 40 were contractors, hired on the basis of their experience with previous versions of the database management system, and its associated development tools. The development process took about two years, and went through a number of small-scale pilots to develop a "proof of concept." After each pilot, more requirements were added.

When development was almost complete, a review was undertaken of the amount of computing power actually required to implement the design. The company discovered, through a simple simulation model of the system, that it would need the entire output of DEC's *VAX* manufacturing plants for two years to get enough computing resources to give adequate response time. They immediately scaled-back the requirement, implemented a much more modest system, and made it work, but in the meantime, they had spent millions of dollars on a project that an early expert review would have pointed out could not be successful.

Decelerator 9. Lack of Business Interest or Business Sponsorship

Description: It will be hard to develop an effective partnership with the business if the business is uninterested in such a partnership or is overly comfortable with the relationship it has now.

Identified by: Citizens' Coke & Gas
E&Y LLP

Observed Effects: Business customers do not want to, and therefore do not try to, participate in an effective partnership. When participation occurs, it is through staff who are not well qualified to act as spokespeople for the business processes that they are supposed to represent. Business sponsors do not see a need to change the way that they operate with regard to the IS organization, because they are not aware that the service provision should or could be better.

Address with: Sponsor education, focusing on the cost of the status quo and the benefits of an effective partnership with the IS organization. Create a few initial successes by whatever means possible, and communicate the additional benefits of effective participation. Identify and recruit the opinion formers and behavior influencers in the business to participate in the partnership. Investigate and introduce incentive programs to reward effective participation.

Comments: Many organizations actually like their IS departments to be passive order-takers. It stops customers from having to participate actively in an area that they do not understand very well and that has a history as a source of problems. It's not that surprising that, in many situations, the customer will not want to join in to the degree that the IS organization wants or needs.

Decelerator 10. Lack of Successes to Copy

Description: If there are no success models, it can be difficult to persuade sponsors to attempt what may be seen to be a risky effort. In the absence of a known route to success, all actions tend to be seen as risky and, as a result, otherwise feasible projects may lack sufficient support to be successful.

Identified by: E&Y LLP

Observed Effects: Organizations that see themselves primarily as followers or late adopters of new approaches are often unwilling to invest in new processes or technologies, unless there are examples of successful adoption that they can study. As a result, they tend to fall behind with their own ability to be successful, and this makes them even more reluctant to invest in emergent ideas. However, if they wait until the approaches they need are widely proven, they may never get the benefits they expect from the investment—their competitors will already have reaped the available benefits and moved on. This is especially true in areas where the benefits appear only over time or areas where there are many false steps reported and few success stories.

Address with: Sponsor education via benchmarking or participative best practices exchanges—often the lack of success is more apparent than real, and moving the focus of research to a new area can discover the successes that inspire the confidence needed to proceed. Improved risk-assessment processes. Leverage can also be obtained from a few well-chosen pilot projects that begin to build a record of successful implementation of new and relatively unproved ideas.

Comments: Care should be taken to ensure that the lack of successes to copy is not a symptom that the IS organization or its customers are attempting something that cannot succeed. Also be aware that, in organizations that choose product innovation as their strategic identity, it will be necessary to create a capability to operate in areas where there are no successful examples.

Decelerator 11. Poor, Missing, or Incomplete Problem Statements

Description: If development projects are allowed to start without clear objectives and well-defined expectations, they will be very unlikely to succeed or to be regarded as successful, even if they deliver what they promise.

Identified by: Citizens' Coke & Gas
E&Y LLP

Observed Effects: In a rush to get started or under pressure to be doing something, IS development projects begin before there is a clear understanding of the objectives for the project. Once they have started, the projects rapidly gain momentum, resources are added and, eventually, deliverables appear. Only then is it realized that the deliverables don't seem to match what the customer wants.

Address with: Improved requirements-analysis processes. Better sponsor education. Management by fact, and awareness-building among IS staff. Development of more appropriate measures of effectiveness and efficiency.

Comments: There is also the possibility that we may have a Type 3 error. When this occurs, although the problem is a real one and the solution that is proposed is workable, the effort is misdirected, because there is a more fundamental problem to solve. Type 3 errors are very common in organizations that do not have an effective strategic partnership with their IS organization.

Decelerator 12. Reskilling Initiatives Are Really Just the Relabeling of Existing Roles

Description: Although there is a continuing rhetoric around reskilling the IS organization, and there may be a continuing investment in education and training, there is no change in work practices, recognition-and-rewards systems, or measurement processes. New skills, when they are actually acquired, are not deployed.

Identified by: E&Y LLP

Observed Effects: Although staff do get trained in new skills and technologies, no attempt is made to leverage this training by actually implementing the new processes or technologies. There may be a limited number of pilot projects, but these never result in widely deployed changes. Staff morale is low, and many staff feel that they are falling behind the industry in terms of what they know how to do. Staff turnover is consequently high unless the IS staff is "captive" because of lack of alternative employment.

Address with: Link skills-development to the implementation of an economies-of-scope program. Develop and deploy a competency model that describes the types and levels of skill that will be required for success in the future. Publish a career-development model and make the preferred development routes clear. Encourage a mixture of foundation-competency development and just-in-time skills acquisition related to project work. Avoid running pilots that, even if successful, cannot lead to any immediate broader deployment.

Comments: Reskilling is one of the key challenges of the 1990s for all IS organizations. Unless a fundamentally new approach is taken to technical and process-competency development, even the best intentioned education and training program will tend to lapse into this situation, over time.

Decelerator 13. Solutions Cannot Be Deployed Rapidly Enough Because the Required Infrastructure Is Not Available

Description: Infrastructure is often difficult to justify in advance, yet takes time to deploy. Projects that will need the infrastructure to be in place and stable before their results can be implemented may not be able to provide sufficient advanced justification for the infrastructure they will need. Deployment must then wait until sufficient infrastructural capacity has been deployed.

Identified by: Ameritech
AT&T
E&Y LLP
Hewlett Packard
Society Corp.

Observed Effects: Development projects are delivered on time and with the necessary functionality, but the infrastructure available can only support limited deployment, either all functions to just a few staff or just a few functions to all staff. Benefits are reduced because of the lack of rapid deployment. Infrastructure implementation is often authorized at this point, but may lag the development process by months or years. Infrastructure integration failures are common as the pressure to deploy grows.

Address with: There are four possible approaches to beating the infrastructure "Catch 22."

The first is the "stealth" infrastructure creation process, where each project inflates its costs slightly and use the surplus to fund essential infrastructure capacity. This has been a common approach for many IS organizations, but has obvious limitations where significant initial investment is required.

The second approach involves collaboration between projects that require substantially the same infrastructure capabilities, but cannot justify them independently. This approach works best where economies-of-scope are already in place. Otherwise, individual projects tend to have too few common requirements.

The third approach involves what we have come to call "act of faith" justification arguments, also commonly called strategic investment decisions.[4] In this approach, an argument based on strategic necessity is used to bypass the normal return-on-investment (ROI) requirements for the investment, because these would fail.

The fourth approach, which has only emerged recently, involves a new funding rationale for infrastructure. Instead of trying to justify infrastructure on the basis of conventional ROI, which almost always fails for the first project that requires the infrastructure, an

[4]In this context, a *strategic investment* is anything that can't be justified in the context for which it is required. Many infrastructure capabilities that will eventually benefit everyone, but initially benefit only a few, get justified this way.

options-pricing model is used. By considering the investment as a "price" to be paid in order to get access to a range of future capabilities, not all of which may actually be needed, we can use the same pricing models used by futures traders to price their products. These models let us calculate a risk-adjusted investment price for the infrastructure we need.

Comments: Implementing a rational process for infrastructure funding is also among the major challenges facing IS organizations. As businesses become more dependent on functioning infrastructure, the pressure increases to make good investments in this area. Infrastructure must be simultaneously stable enough to provide predictable levels of performance and flexible enough to accommodate the constantly changing technological capabilities that we will want to incorporate into it.

Decelerator 14. Systems-Integration Requirements Exceed the Available Technical Capabilities

Description: In many cases, the degree of systems-integration effort required to successfully implement both development and delivery environments is beyond the capabilities and experience of the IS organization. Although there is much experimentation and strong sponsorship for trying new things, nothing is ever widely implemented or used for more than one project. The IT organization does nothing but "pilot" projects. There is a continuing technology chase, but little is ever widely adopted. There are too many technology solutions looking for business problems. Communication of the knowledge and experience gained from pilot projects or technology integration trials does not occur.

Identified by: E&Y LLP
IBM
Xerox
Citizens' Coke & Gas
Georgia Pacific

Observed Effects: There is no coherent framework within which to select and integrate technology. Technologies are selected on a project-by-project basis without regard to the integration costs or possibilities. Integration failures are common, and there is a "patchwork" of intermediate applications and "utilities" that stitches applications together, although the results are unstable and require constant adjustment. Significant amounts of time are spent on data-rationalization issues. Application behaviors vary from place to place and application to application. There is a continuing high training cost for both the IS organization and its customers.

Address with: Infrastructure planning and demand management. A simplification program to reduce the number of technologies in use and to build-up integration skills in the selected set. Development of an integration capability either in-house or in collaboration with one or more third parties who have similar problems. Outsourcing, to create access to a critical mass of skills, can be considered, but may be only marginally effective unless other initiatives are undertaken.

Comments: Systems-integration with distributed computing technologies is from two to ten times more complex than with host-centric architectures, and requires from five to 25 times as much resources. An application will typically require 40 "products" for complete implementation. There will usually be around 25 different vendors involved. Version release schedules will not be coordinated and vendors will not test their products with each other prior to shipping them to customers. The number of combinations that must be tested is simply too large. Hence, customers do the integration testing for their vendors. This is an expensive and time-consuming process, even if you plan for it and invest in a capability to do it.

Decelerator 15. Demands for Cross-Functional Sponsorship Cannot Be Met

Description: Not enough of the essential business participants are willing to join in a common effort to create the necessary partnerships with the IS organization.

Identified by: Apple
E&Y LLP
Hewlett Packard
IBM
McDonald's

Observed Effects: Despite well-intentioned attempts to form cross-functional teams, some groups of business users will not participate to the extent required for the teams to be effective. Executive sponsors in some parts of the business have agendas that run counter to the efforts of the IS organization, and there is insufficient high-level sponsorship to gain their compliance.

Address with: Sponsor education. Limited-scope projects that deliver significant benefits without such broad participation. Improved information-sharing.

Comments: In most change situations there will be those who perceive themselves as losers if the change becomes widespread and successful. If those who think they will lose as a result of the change are in sponsoring positions, they can effectively sabotage the change effort by a refusal to participate. They will usually have a reasonable excuse for non-participation, but are, in reality, hoping that the change will fail and they will benefit by not being associated with it.

Decelerator 16. The Human Resource (HR) Organization Cannot Adapt to Changing Needs for Reward-and-Recognition Systems

Description: In many cases, otherwise worthwhile change efforts will fail because the HR organization cannot respond with appropriate advice and support.

Identified by: E&Y LLP
Georgia Pacific
Waste Management

Observed Effects: Despite the development of new reward-and-recognition systems and performance-measurement processes by IS management, the new systems and measures cannot be introduced because the HR organization cannot make the necessary changes to its management systems. A desire for uniformity in assessment and compensation systems prevents effective incentive programs from being developed and deployed.

Address with: Sponsor education. Benchmarking. It may, in extreme cases, be necessary for the IS organization to petition senior business management for permission to create its own HR function.

Comments: We have observed this problem many times and in many organizations. It is usually worst in large hierarchically structured organizations and machine bureaucracies where a uniform HR process is highly valued and any attempt to deviate from the standard process is immediately resisted. Where the HR function reports to the CFO rather than the COO there is a high probability that this decelerator will be present. Because the intelligent use of recognition-and-reward systems to provide incentive for changed behavior is a major lever for effective change management, this decelerator has a disproportionately damaging effect whenever it is present. Unless it is possible for staff to see the difference in recognition and reward between the desired new behavior and not changing behavior at all, why should anyone change?

Decelerator 17. The Wrong Measures of Success Are Being Used

Description: Since, in general, you will get what you measure, if you measure the wrong things you will usually get the wrong outcomes. For instance, if utilization is the only measure of performance, where is the incentive to improve productivity?

Identified by: E&Y LLP

Observed Effects: Staff work toward getting a good value for the measures that they believe their managers take notice of, whether or not these are related to the expressed objectives of the processes that they are being asked to adopt.

Address with: Better measurement design. Sponsor education. Staff education and continued communication programs. Development and use of representative performance indicators that support the desired process and behavior changes.

Comments: Designing measurement programs is not easy, and a bad program is a major barrier to rapid improvement. Ideally, we would like a single measurement process to satisfy all manner of different metrics. In practice this is too optimistic a view. It is better to select one or two appropriate measures from each area of the balanced scorecard and tune these to the needs of the improvement process.[5] If the measurement process is appropriate and the measures well designed, the cost of measurement will be small in relation to the benefit gained.

Decelerator 18. There Are Clear Priority Conflicts in the Many "Strategic" Initiatives

Description: The introduction of too many initiatives and the setting of too many priorities dissipate energy and enthusiasm, even when all the initiatives are well aligned with strategic objectives. Often they are not even partly aligned.

Identified by: Eli Lilly
E&Y LLP

Observed Effects: There are many simultaneous initiatives without a clear theme and with no obvious synergy. Priorities conflict with each other and change frequently. Nothing ever gets finished. More initiatives are introduced on a regular basis, whether or not previous initiatives have been successful or are even complete. Objectives are often in conflict with each other or with past efforts. No one seems to be setting an overall direction.

Address with: Portfolio assessment and priority rationalization. "Top Ten" lists and the setting of realistic expectations. Sponsor education. Effective measurement programs.

Comments: We heard the perfect description of this situation from a colleague based in California who had recently joined E&Y LLP

[5] For more information on the use of the balanced scorecard in effective measurement program design, see Charles Gold's TQM-IS Research Note, *IS Measures—A Balancing Act*, May 1992, available from the Ernst & Young Center for Business Innovation, One Walnut Street, Boston MA 02108.

from Federal Express. She described this situation as the "BOHICA" position. BOHICA stands for "Bend Over Here It Comes Again." This accurately describes the attitude that is soon established when it is clear that the organization is operating in *priority du jour* mode.

Decelerator 19. There Is No Support for the Implementation of Corporate Policies or Initiatives

Description: Even though staff and managers are told to "get things done," no resources are made available to achieve the implementation for which they are apparently responsible. No one is willing to support the necessary efforts. Accountability and/or responsibility without capability is a common situation. In many cases, this situation has persisted for long enough that there is no real accountability for performance at the executive level, either.

Identified by: Eli Lilly
E&Y LLP

Observed Effects: There is profound cynicism among IS staff and managers regarding executive commitment to change because actions do not match words. No one "walks the talk" in a meaningful way. IS staff feel that they will get blamed for their failure to improve, even though the improvements they are required to make need investments that they are prevented from making. Staff morale is low and turnover is high. Many staff adopt a "low profile," hoping that the constant criticism will wash over them and leave them personally unaffected so long as they seem busy.

Address with: Sponsor education and management. Management by fact. The presence of an effective performance-measurement program can do a great deal to demonstrate the need for focused investment in support of improvement programs.

Comments: While it is easy for a CEO or CIO to declare, "We will become more productive," that does not make the improvements happen. Some degree of investment is almost always necessary to carry-through the improvement program. Although the relative impact of the decision to change may be small at the top of the IS organization, it gets increasingly large as we move through the line managers, project managers, and staff. Decisions that can be made by an executive team in minutes may take months or years to implement when applied to the whole organization. If there is a lack of realism in the initiating executive's view of the implementation effort, the implementation will fail.

Decelerator 20. There Is "Too Much to Know" to Get Everything Right That Needs to Be Right

Description: The number of essential sets of knowledge exceed the skills and experience available within the IS organization and its customers. Key skill combinations are not available in sufficient numbers to provide the required change projects or development pathfinders. The communication of knowledge and experience does not occur.

Identified by: E&Y LLP
IBM

Observed Effects: There are many false starts with projects because some essential aspect is missing through ignorance. Teams often assume that they can leverage past skills and experience to a much greater extent than is, in fact, possible. This results in many blind alleys and much rework. There is a tendency to blame the new technologies (which are often, in part, culpable) and an unwillingness to admit that the new competency requirements have not yet been met.

Address with: Awareness-building. Coaching by experts. Focused reskilling programs and just-in-time training. Competency-building and certification programs. The collection of examples and best practices from outside sources.

Comments: Developing for the newer distributed computing technologies is complex and requires developers to be aware of many aspects of infrastructure that were hidden from the application in host-centric environments. Learning curves are steep, and there is a high critical mass of knowledge that must be available before a project can be successful.

Decelerator 21. There Is a Lack of Clear Requirements Or of a Basis on Which to Assign Them

Description: There is a constant and uncontrolled explosion of customer requirements. Customer participation in projects changes frequently. There is no identified customer sponsor for the work.

Identified by: Eli Lilly

Observed Effects: It is difficult to get customer agreement to key project milestones. Development-and-delivery dates slip as critical issues fail to be resolved quickly, or at all. "Revolving door" requirements appear, and a backlog of conflicting requirements grows without resolution.[6] Requirements analysis never ends, or is declared complete with an incomplete solution design in place. Prototypes constantly precipitate additional requirements. There is a mismatch between features and functionality in the proposed solution.

Address with: Sponsor education and management. Cross-functional teams. Specification by example and prototyping.

Comments: A good strategy in this situation is often to stop the project and wait to see who complains. If no one complains, we can move on to more important work. If someone emerges as a real customer, we can start to build effective sponsorship for their requirements. Once a real sponsor has been identified, we can set up an effective issue-resolution and priority-assessment mechanism and try to move forward. Lack of consistent customer input is a common symptom of a Type 3 error, or a badly misstated business problem.

Decelerator 22. Threat to the Current IS Power/Influence Structures

Description: The organizational levels at which the pain of the status quo is most acutely perceived may not be the ones needed to legitimize or implement the necessary changes. Those who are required to sponsor the changes, and whose involvement is critical during the transitional period, are likely to be the losers if the change occurs.

[6] A "revolving door" requirement occurs when customer A wants something, but is then replaced as a source of requirements by customer B, who wants the opposite. Customer B is, in turn, replaced by customer C, who returns to the original requirements, and so on.

Identified by: E&Y LLP
Farmers Insurance
McDonald's
Sabre Travel Information Network

Observed Effects: Overt or covert resistance at the sponsor or executive level. Adverse propaganda regarding the probability of success for the improvement program. Refusal to participate. The creation and pursuit of "alternative" change agendas that actually seek to maintain the status quo. Downplaying of any benefits that are achieved, usually by claims that "we would have gained that improvement anyway." Isolation of those involved in the change effort and marginalization of their efforts.

Address with: Sponsor education and management. Awareness-building.

Comments: In the most extreme cases, it may be necessary to move, or remove, the executives who are the focus of the problem, and live with the transitional consequences.

Decelerator 23. Too Many Changes Are Required for the Improvements to Succeed

Description: The future state is so different from the current state that even those who wish to make the change may exhaust their capacity to do so in the time frame needed to achieve the required improvements.

Identified by: E&Y LLP

Observed Effects: As the amount of required change exceeds an individual's or a group's capacity to assimilate the change, dysfunctional behavior begins to appear. This may take many forms, among which, covert resistance and current state advocacy, are common. Momentum is lost from the change process as individuals or teams spend more and more time on finding reasons not to change. Eventually, no further change occurs, and the level of dysfunctional behavior may also reduce the effectiveness of the original state that everyone is seeking to preserve.

Address with: Awareness-building and change-target education. Increased incentives to adopt changed processes and behaviors. Better management of the pace of change. Better focused change-agent activity. Sponsor education and management.

Comments: This is an insidious problem. Our observations indicate that as few as 30 percent of IS staff make the required changes in a reasonably short time. Of the remainder, perhaps half (35 percent) will make the change if assisted, albeit much more slowly. The last 35 percent may never make the change successfully. The management challenge arises when more than the initial 30 percent of converts are required to create a functioning future-state organization.

Decelerator 24. Too Much Reliance Is Placed on a Few Key Individuals for Them to Be Effective as Change Agents

Description: Isolated practitioners get stale if they cannot interact with their peers. Substitution of one person for another becomes difficult, because the organization depends on the individual, not the role. Experience is not leveraged between change agents. Communication of knowledge and experience does not occur.

Identified by: Citizens' Coke & Gas
E&Y LLP

Observed Effects: Change agents become too involved in the process with which they work, and lose sight of the overall objectives of the change. There is a steady dropoff in the levels of attention paid to the essential tasks of sponsor education and management. There is an increase in activity related to items of concern over which the change agent has no influence.

Address with: Improved change-agent training and awareness-building. Performance-support systems for change agents and coaching facilities. Use of outside coaches if necessary. Creation and use of a change-agent peer group, using Groupware and "virtual" knowledge sharing, if necessary. Careful evaluation of change-agent performance to detect early signs of ineffective behavior.

Comments: It is often difficult to teach change agents the difference between agent behavior and advocacy. If change agents spend too much of their time and energy addressing areas over which they have no influence, they will be increasingly frustrated and ineffective. If they have no access to a peer group that can point out the problem, it will probably go unaddressed until the change agent is completely ineffective.

Decelerator 25. Use of Successes Elsewhere That Can't Be Repeated

Description: This is a very discouraging situation. Benchmarking can lead an organization to try to adopt practices that have been successful elsewhere, but these practices can fail for a variety of reasons. Usually the problem is one of misjudging context—not understanding why a success occurred where and when it did, and hence not providing the necessary success factors for the adoption to succeed.

Identified by: AT&T
E&Y LLP

Observed Effects: Initial enthusiasm for the change quickly dissipates as unexpected problems crop-up. Energy is wasted and expectations fail to be met. Sponsorship quickly evaporates. Blame is commonly placed on either the source of the practice or on those who planned the implementation.

Address with: Improved benchmarking processes. More realistic expectation setting for the change process. Pilot adoption programs to "debug" the implementation process and identify critical success factors. Sponsor education. Better implementation planning.

Comments: Another manifestation of the "Silver Bullet" myth. Understanding why a practice or process works in one place takes time and effort, which may be begrudged if the practice is especially attractive because of its perceived utility and success. Translating the understanding into actions that support adoption of the practice elsewhere often makes what appeared to be a "quick fix" a much harder task. In reality there are very few quick fixes available.

In a small number of situations, we have encountered businesses or groups that actively encourage their less-effective competitors to adopt apparently effective practices because the leaders know that the followers will not be able to make them work, and will fall further behind as a result of trying.

9

Implementing a Cycle Time Reduction Program

Only the paranoid survive.[1]

Chapters 6, 7, and 8 have provided the basis for developing a cycle time improvement and productivity improvement program. Now let's look at an actual example. This chapter contains an example program for the IS organization of a fictitious company, ABC Inc. The material in this chapter is based on an amalgam of several actual programs we have developed for a variety of clients, with the content suitably modified to exclude anything that related solely to the unique circumstances of the individual clients of the original programs. It is illustrative of the kind of programmatic template with which we typically begin the development of a multi-project, multi-year improvement process.

ABC Inc. has approximately 250 development-and-delivery staff in the IS organization. Staff are all centrally managed and co-located in a separate building from their customers. The IS staff support all new development projects (there are usually 5 or 6 new projects each year) and undertake the maintenance or enhancement of all existing applications and packages. ABC Inc. has a substantial suite of legacy applications, including several large packages, running on a mainframe computer. In reaction to customer demand, the IS organization has been introducing distributed computing applications and local area networks for the last three years. ABC's users (of which there are about 3,200) have all been converted over to PCs, many of which also emulate terminals to access older applications when required. The IS application development and maintenance budget is currently around $30 million and is required to decrease by 10 percent per year for the next two years.

The improvement program has as its object the reduction in cycle time of the IS development-and-delivery process by 20 to 25 percent each year for three years and a corresponding improvement in productivity from the IS development-and-delivery resources of

[1]Quoted from a speech by Andy Groves, CEO of Intel.

18 to 23 percent per year. At the same time, costs must be reduced by 10 percent per year. These are fairly typical objectives for an improvement program, by no means as aggressive as is possible, nor trivial to achieve.

The IS organization in our example measures productivity in resource hours per delivered function point (FP) for new development projects, and uses an analogous "maintenance point" (MP) for measuring maintenance productivity. Cycle times are measured from project initiation to acceptance by the sponsoring users.

A significant part of the IS department's work is the implementation and continuing support of five large software packages. The packages normally get a new version release every 18 months and there are typically 30 to 40 "fixes" that must be incorporated between each release.

There are also many small development and enhancement projects, typically taking less than 100 staff hours each.

The baseline values for productivity and cycle time, produced from the results of retrospective analysis and a three-month detailed survey of IS activity, are given in Table 9.1, along with the corresponding annual improvement target values.

The percentage improvements required imply a doubling of productivity with the three years of the program, and a more than halving of cycle times.

Because the improvement benefits will require considerable process change, it is a requirement of the approach that the IS organization be given one three-month period in each year to "rest and recuperate" and absorb the necessary changes. Thus the program will plan change projects only in three out of four quarters each year. Also, because the improvement objectives represent a year-on-year comparison, and improvements will not appear immediately, actual program targets must be greater than the objective values in order to get the required average improvements.

Table 9.1 *Example Baseline Productivity and Cycle Time Figures, with Targets for a Three-Year Improvement Program*

	Baseline	Year 1	Year 2	Year 3
Average resource hours per function point for large projects (>1000 FP)	21	16.8	13.4	10.7
Resource hours per function point for small projects (<1000 FP)	14	11.2	9	7.2
Resource hours per function point for ad hoc projects (<50 FP)	10	8	6.4	5.1
Hours per maintenance point (internally developed software)	31	24.8	19.8	15.9
Hours per maintenance point (packages)	37	29.6	23.7	18.9
Hours per small-change project (<20 maintenance points)	135	108	86.4	69.1
Cycle Time: Large projects (in weeks)	50	37.5	28	21
Cycle Time: Small projects (in weeks)	34	25.5	19	14.5
Cycle Time: Ad hoc projects (in days)	11	8.5	6	4.5
Cycle Time: Maintenance projects (in weeks)	21	16	12	9
Cycle Time: Package-enhancement projects (in weeks)	26	19.5	14.5	11
Cycle Time: Small-change projects (in days)	13	10	7.5	5.5

The Assessment

We start the assessment by defining the key characteristics of a high-performing IS organization. These characteristics were developed from research and assessments that we have accumulated over several years of actual improvement efforts and research. There is a more substantial discussion of the characteristics in our earlier work, *Development Effectiveness: Strategies for IS Organizational Transition.*[2]

We look at seven important aspects of the IS organization:

1. Mission
2. Culture
3. Organization
4. IT processes
5. Customer interface
6. Infrastructure
7. Economics

Next, we assess how well our company's IS organization scores in each of these seven critical areas. Table 9.2 shows an example of the simple data collection instrument we commonly use.

We normally carry out this initial assessment from both the IS organization's (internal) and customer's satisfaction (external) viewpoints. Analyzing the resulting differences in perception (which are always there to some degree) is the first part of our awareness-building program, aimed at creating a justification for improvement and an agenda for change within the IS organization.

Next we quantify the areas where we can have the most impact from our performance-improvement efforts. Table 9.3 shows the typical relative proportions of effort associated with each of the IS work categories (task types) for each of the process segments that we will aim to improve at ABC Inc. Note that we have excluded

[2] *Development Effectiveness: Strategies for IS Organizational Transition,* Chapter 3, by Vaughn Merlyn and John Parkinson. New York: John Wiley & Sons, 1994.

Table 9.2 *Example of an Initial Assessment Instrument*

		ABC Inc.	Comment
Mission	Cannot exist in isolation		
	Cannot rest on past successes		
	Cannot assume that it cannot or need not do better		
Culture	Values excellence		
	Is resilient to high levels of change		
	Values and rewards judicious experimentation		
	Understands that individuals play different roles		
	Recognizes the value of both skills and competencies		
	Accepts and encourages objective measures of performance		
	Encourages the acquisition and dissemination of new learning		
	Promotes values of openness and receptivity		
Organization	Customer-focused		
	Development, assembly and delivery oriented		
	Infrastructure management and provisioning		

Table 9.2 *(Continued)*

		ABC Inc.	Comment
	Program and project sponsoring		
	Technology-enablement group		
IT Processes	Process Specialization		
	Delivery Flexibility		
	Focus on the Future		
	Continuous Improvement		
	Process Maturity		
Customer Interface	Participation		
	Responsiveness		
	Consideration for the Customer		
Infrastructure	Automation		
	Reuse		
	Performance Support		
Economics	Focus on Business Value		
	Demonstrates Tactical Cost Effectiveness		
	Recognizes Strategic Investment Needs		

the work associated with very small projects and enhancements, because this will not meet our coverage and improvement potential criteria.

Table 9.3 *Distribution of Effort among IS Development-and-Delivery Staff at ABC Inc.*

	New Develop-ment (FP-based)	Application Enhance-ment (MP-based)	Package Installa-tion	Required Maintenance of Packages
Discovery and the Use of Past Experience	20	10	10	5
Problem Analysis and Modeling	10	40	10	25
Solution Identification and Selection	20	15	25	20
Deliverable Creation and Installation	30	20	30	30
Communication	5	5	5	5
Implementation	5	5	10	10
Process Management	10	5	10	5
Total	100	100	100	100

Opportunities for Improvement

The basic formula[3] for assessing improvements in process productivity, or determining the Productivity Index (PI), is:

$$PI = 1/[(1 - k - j) + k/m - n/j]$$

[3]This formula is derived from original work by Professor Guido Dedene, carried out at the University of Leiden, with funding from the IBM Share Group.

where

k = proportion of the work made better by the improvement ($k \leqslant 1$)

j = the proportion of the work made worse by the improvement ($j \leqslant 1$)($k + j \leqslant 1$)

$(1 - k - j)$ = the proportion of the work not affected by the improvement, and

m = the degree to which the affected work is improved (m must be > 0).

n = the degree to which the affected work gets worse (n must be $\geqslant 0$

$m = n = 1$ implies no change since $k/m = k$, $j/n = j$ and $[(1 - k - j) + k + j] = 1$.

For now, we will simplify the argument by assuming that $n = 0$, that is, no improvement that we attempt makes the productivity of any part of the remaining work worse. In practice, so long as $k >> j$ and $m >> n$ this simplification is good enough.

From this we can see that, as m gets larger, k/m tends to zero and the formula tends to $1/[1 - k]$. In essence, therefore, the improvement we can achieve is determined mostly by the *coverage* of the change—*not by the degree of change being made*. Note also that, if we assume that the effects of multiple improvement actions are simply additive (in general, this is a good first approximation), we can apply the formula successively to get a cumulative assessment of the result to be expected from a number of related initiatives.

To calculate the percent of resources saved for any given combination of k and m, we invert the PI and subtract the result from 1. Then convert to a percent:

$$\% \text{ Resources Reduced (PRR)} = (1 - (1/\text{PI})) * 100$$

We can easily develop a simple spreadsheet to calculate this productivity index and the associated percent reduction in resources. With this in mind, we need to focus improvement initiatives on areas that affect as much of the work at ABC Inc. as possible—and, in consequence, as many IS resources as possible.

This is more difficult where the range of types of work is broad, with a relatively small proportion of people working on any specific set of activities. We will need to focus on areas that are common to all work types where this is possible and, where it is not, to have multiple initiatives that together provide the coverage we seek.

Demand Management

Demand management initiatives seek to manipulate the demand stream toward solutions that can be delivered efficienty by ABC Inc. IS resources. This means, in part, simplifying the range of technologies that must be employed (and then maintained) to deliver solutions and, in part, developing a better solution value model with the customer. IS staff can then work to optimize the extension, management, and support of the current application portfolio by, for example, replacing older or costly to maintain applications with more cost-efficient solutions as a part of continuing enhancement or required maintenance work. In essence, the IS organization will seek to exercise more control over how solutions are delivered—not to determine what solutions are required.

Effective demand management would also work toward allowing a more effective scheduling of IS resources to match the pattern of solution development and delivery negotiated with ABC Inc. internal customers on a period-by-period basis.

Process

The IS development processes at ABC Inc. do not yet exhibit the defined, repeatable, measured characteristics needed for significant process leverage. Work on process specialization and tailoring can be undertaken, but work would be required for each of the disparate process areas required to support current IS activity. Until demand management can reduce the range of processes or process variants that must be employed, there are a limited number of common process-related areas that could be the focus of short-term improvement initiatives.

Project (and some aspects of process) management is such an area. Addressing this area has a number of added advantages:

- It affects all the types of work done by the IS organization (every project must be managed), but involves a relatively small group of key staff so that the change-management issues can be more readily addressed.
- It can be used to exemplify the benefits to be derived from the application of a defined, repeatable process in a disciplined manner. Establishing the connection between use of a disciplined management process and productive working is an important success factor in internalizing better execution discipline among all staff.
- Routinely excellent project management is a continuing critical success factor for the deployment of an improved and continuously improving process.

A second area where broad process improvements can be initiated involves the provision of additional performance-support capabilities. By capturing and making available value added knowledge and key practices, examples, and experience, practitioners can provide mutual leverage to their colleagues, reduce errors causing rework, and simplify issue resolution by ensuring that the correct people are involved.

A third area for broad improvements to all processes covers further development of process measurement and associated metrication (analysis of measurement data) to drive further non-programmatic process-improvement opportunities).

Technology

The degree to which technology can be successfully deployed to assist with process improvements is also related to the simplification of supported platform technologies. Until this occurs, it will be difficult to identify areas where the numbers of people whose efforts are leveraged by new technology is sufficiently large to justify the investment in the technology. There are a number of areas where this possibility exists, however, and these should be investigated. For example:

- The modeling of requirements for new applications and for major enhancements.
- Program structure understanding for enhancements and required maintenance.
- Design, construction, and testing integration for mainframe-based applications development and required maintenance using high-performance development environment (HPDE) concepts.
- Unit, integration, and system testing for new applications, application enhancement, and required maintenance.
- Version and configuration management.

In addition, a number of infrastructure technology capabilities should be developed to support the broadly based improvement initiatives around: performance support; shared experience capture and deployment; and knowledge sharing.

People

Organizational Change Management teaches us that an individual's ability to assimilate change is limited. If this limit is exceeded, dysfunctional behaviors of various types will result. This has two implications for a continuing program of improvement initiatives:

1. The program should not try to introduce too many radical changes in process or environment that might trigger widespread dysfunctional responses.
2. As far as possible, the program should incorporate periods of stability where changes are kept to a minimum and the benefits from past changes can begin to accumulate in a visible way.

A protracted period of change and the expectation that change will continue to be necessary both generate high levels of ambiguity in the working environment for IS staff. Although much of this ambiguity is unavoidable, it must still be properly managed. Improvement initiatives should therefore focus on reinforcing areas where change has already occurred, but is not yet internalized, as well as further strengthening the ability of IS staff to cope with ambiguity through communication, education, mentoring, and similar support programs.

Some continuing changes will, however, be required and these should, as far as possible, focus on the development of the behaviors required for a successful, disciplined process that can be used by all staff as a model of what is expected of them.

There remains a final issue related to the people dimension. A balance must be achieved between the need to move all IS staff forward in terms of their ability to be more productive, and a reward-and-recognition program that distinguishes those individuals and groups that best exhibit the behaviors we seek to deploy. We may seek, for the time being, to avoid overt disincentives, but a program to provide incentive for desired behaviors should be considered.

Year 1 Improvement Initiatives

Recommended Strategy/Approach

This section describes the set of initiatives that might be proposed for the first year of the cycle time improvement program to meet the performance targets for ABC Inc.'s IS organization. The program is organized into four focus areas:

1. Demand Management
2. Process Management
3. Process Execution
4. Infrastructure Provisioning

Within each of these areas, we have classified individual projects as focused on initiatives that are:

- Process related
- People related
- Technology related

This gives us a 4 × 3 matrix within which to organize each year's projects.

Year 1 Performance Improvement Program: Proposed Initiatives

Demand-Management-Related Portfolio

Process-Related Initiatives

Initiative	***New Option-Appraisal Process for IS Development Proposals***
Description:	Discuss an option-appraisal process that allows the IS organization to offer solution proposals that focus on existing or preferred technology sets and limit the number of new technologies that must be introduced and subsequently supported.
Scope:	Potentially affects all current IS processes but would be unlikely to eliminate any currently supported technology sets in Year 1.
Number of staff affected:	Approximately 100 in Year 1
Potential impact:	Year 1: No new technologies introduced. Identify and implement at least five replacement/improvement initiatives in current portfolio (application enhancement or required maintenance).

Comments: This is more of an initiative to establish a new set of operating principles than a specific program to implement demand management. Nevertheless, opportunities to simplify the support workload and improve maintenance effectiveness do exist if the IS organization can be involved in the proposal or selection of solution options.

People-Related Initiatives

Initiative: ***Skills Profiles and Future Skills Demand Model***

Description: Build a profile of currently available skills, and map these to future state demand model for ABC Inc.'s IS staffing. Prepare a gap analysis and a migration plan. Map the desired migration to the business model for future years and factor the results as inputs to a Year 2 process change program initiative.

Scope: All current IS processes

Number of staff affected: All current IS staff

Potential impact: Year 1: May offer the opportunity to better match available skills and career-development programs to meet the current pattern of demand. There should be a potential for scheduling improvements in resource allocation but not (probably) raw productivity improvements.

Comments: Can be built-up into a long-term career and competency development program.

Technology-Related Initiatives

Initiative ***No New Platform Technologies***

Description: Agree with ABC Inc. customers that there will be no new technology sets introduced during 1994.

Scope: New FP-based development

Number of staff affected: c. 120

Potential impact: Year 1: No direct impact, but no new investments required in training and learning curve productivity losses.

Comments: Another holding initiative, but an important one, paving the way for reductions in later years. Also a demonstration of the desire to stabilize development and maintenance processes.

Process Management-Related Portfolio

Process-Related Initiatives

Initiative ***Standardize Project Structuring & Planning***

Description: Deploy a standard project structuring and planning process to all projects. Specialize use of the process by project type and develop template project plans for common projects. Implement a formal and rigorous project charter review process.

Scope: All projects

Number of staff affected: All project managers (40)

Potential impact: Year 1: 16%, based on research averages
Year 2: 6%–9% through continuous improvement
Year 3: 6%–9% through continuous improvement

Comments: Builds on work to develop and deploy specific project charter templates and processes.

Initiative ***Process Measurement***

Description: Introduce and deploy an activity-measurement program that captures time actually spent by task for all staff, so that an activity analysis can

	be undertaken and sources of non-value-added and unplanned work can be identified and addressed.
Scope:	All IS processes
Number of staff affected:	All IS staff
Potential impact:	Year 1: We can anticipate an initial Hawthorne Effect improvement (although in some "measure aware" environments, this may be reduced) followed by process tuning and improvement actions. Evidence from elsewhere indicates that a cumulative productivity gain of 10 percent should be possible in the first year. Year 2: Subsequent gains occur as a result of quantitatively directed process-improvement actions and improved staff capability to role mapping. Improvements should average 6% per year. Year 3: Assume a continuing 6% per year average gain.
Comments:	Aims primarily at control of unplanned work. Also a necessary precursor to process improvements in Year 2 and to a more flexible recognition/reward system.

People-Related Initiatives

Initiative	***Project Management Training and Coaching***
Description:	A continuing program of education, coaching, and support for the project management group in the IS organization, focusing on disciplined compliance with the project structuring, planning, and management processes.
Scope:	All project managers and team leaders across all IT process types
Number of staff affected:	All project managers and team leaders (70)

Potential impact: Year 1: Small work-related gains for the project managers themselves, but large potential for the efficiency of managed projects.

Comments: Supports deployment and reinforcement of best practices for Project Management.

Initiative: ***Performance Incentives Program Pilots***

Description: A pilot program to design and implement a recognition-and-reward scheme that differentiates those individuals and teams that exhibit the behaviors and characteristics that we wish to reinforce.

Scope: A single IS process type initially (Year 1), followed by deployment to all process types (Year 2).

Number of staff affected: 50 staff in Year 1. Everyone in IS by Year 3.

Potential impact: Year 1: Target of 15% in the affected group
Year 2: Target of 10% in everyone

Comments: Try an incentives-only program initially but prepare an explicit sanctions program as possible reinforcement later if required.

Technology-Related Initiatives

Initiative ***Project Planning and Structuring Tools***

Description: Ensure that all project managers have adequate and unrestricted access to the project structuring and planning tools provided for their use.

Scope: All project managers

Number of staff affected: 40

Potential impact: Year 1: Small resource gain for the project managers involved, but significant potential for efficiency gains in actual projects once standardized planning process is used and options can be easily examined before a final plan is adopted.

Comments: The 16 percent to 24 percent resource gains from specialized project-planning approaches can only be achieved if the support tools are used in a disciplined and standardized fashion.

Process Execution-Related Portfolio

Process-Related Initiatives

Initiative ***Standardize Core IT Processes***

Description: Ensure that all new projects in each process type use a common baseline when designing project plans and that all projects execute to this baseline.

Scope: All process types

Number of staff affected: All staff involved in new projects

Potential impact: Year 1: Reduction in rework through reduction in process variations. Preparation for process execution focus in Year 2.

Comments: This will be a secondary initiative in Year 1, but will react opportunistically as each new project is chartered, leveraging the Project Management initiatives to ensure that project team members are aware of the process they should be following and that there are incentives for those who demonstrate compliance to the standard process.

Initiative ***Identify a Small Number of High-Impact Areas Focus for Specific Improvement Actions***

Description: Identify a small number of areas of current practice where an improvement action would have a high payback and implement appropriate actions.

Scope: Depends on findings

Number of staff affected: Likely to be relatively small initially

Potential impact: Year 1: Target is 40% in selected areas
Comments: Examples would be the vendor relationship management and version acceptance and integration aspects of package maintenance.

Initiative ***Defect Source Analysis***
Description: Record and examine the root cause of all reported defects for a period of time (probably at least three months). Develop and deploy a program of improvement actions to reduce or eliminate the source of defects.
Scope: All IT process types
Number of staff affected: Potentially all IS staff
Potential impact: Year 1: 35% reduction in introduced defects
Comments: This is an essential process quality assessment step in designing a continuing program of process-improvement initiatives. Results depend on what is found and the speed with which root causes can be addressed within the rest of the improvement program.

Initiative ***Utilization Monitoring Review***
Description: Record and investigate the root cause of unproductive work and unplanned work across all IS projects. Consider the development of a resource scheduling simulation model with which to investigate schedule optimization opportunities.
Scope: All IS projects
Number of staff affected: All staff
Potential impact: Year 1: Probably low, but a potential of 10 percent has been seen elsewhere when complex multi-demand scheduling across a varied resource pool is required.

Comments: This project looks at the efficiency with which IS resources are scheduled across the demand for IS-supplied services. Although there may be little opportunity to improve the allocation of resources to demand in the short term, a medium-term improvement program should look at dynamic resource scheduling as a potential source of further productivity through optimizing utilization.

Initiative ***Introduce Formal Change-Management and Issue-Management Processes***

Description: Ensure that all projects document, evaluate, and manage scope of work changes in a disciplined fashion.

Scope: All projects

Number of staff affected: All staff

Potential impact: Year 1: Experience suggests that a 15%–20% improvement is available by more rigorous vetting of change requests and better version control.

Comments: There is a sense that change-management and issue-management processes lack the discipline that has been established in other areas of the development process.

People-Related Initiatives

Initiative ***Coaching***

Description: Continue the coaching and mentoring schemes provided by the process-improvement staff. Plan to create and support a second level of coaches from within the IS resource pool. Look for and "recruit" individuals who can act as front-line process coaches and who will be the focus for process discipline within project teams.

Scope: On demand, measure the coverage of the program and investigate under/over supply situations.

Number of staff affected: All IS staff

Potential impact: Year 1: Target is a 15 percent productivity improvement through learning curve reduction and deployment of best practices.

Comments: Coaching is an effective way to leverage skilled resources over a group of less skilled staff, provided that the coaches are selected for coaching capability and the coaching group is integrated into the working processes of IS as a whole. External coaches are a good way to get the program started, and remain an effective support capability, but for long-term success, internal coaching skills must be identified and deployed.

Initiative ***Process Awareness***

Description: Develop and deploy a series of IS process-awareness classes/workshops to ensure that all IS staff understand the key concepts of the development process and have the opportunity to ask questions where they are uncertain as to how the process applies to their areas of work.

Scope: All IT process types

Number of staff affected: All IS staff

Potential impact: Year 1: Eliminate time lost due to lack of familiarity with the expected process. Estimate a 5 percent net saving.

Comments: Staff can only be effective with the disciplined processes required for sustained high productivity if they understand how the work they carry out fits into the overall development and maintenance processes that IS organization is using. Education in the nature and demands of these processes is an effective way to focus attention on the behaviors that will deliver effective working practices, process improvements, and sustainable efficiencies of execution.

Technology-Related Initiatives

Initiative	***LAN-Based Performance Support***
Description:	Develop and deploy a LAN-based common repository of useful knowledge and value-added reference material that supports the work of all IS staff.
Scope:	All IS processes
Number of staff affected:	All IS staff
Potential impact:	Year 1: Reduce or eliminate time spent searching for help or reference materials. Reduce or eliminate time spent on rework due to lack of access to advice, examples, or the correct process descriptions. Reduce or eliminate rework due to process failures caused by lack of access to critical advice or existing best practices. Cumulative first-year effect could be 10 percent of total resources.
Comments:	Where many new practices are involved, staff often are uncertain as to what they should do in specific circumstances. If advice is not readily available, process errors can occur that soon become working practices, even though a better practice is available. Easy access to performance support information can control this tendency.

Initiative	***High Performance Development Environment (HPDE) Research***
Description:	There are a number of areas where the use of an integrated tool set to support an IT process

	could be beneficial, but, because of the diversity of current processes, the leverage to be gained from technology-led improvements needs to be carefully examined prior to the decision to invest. This project looks at areas where the resource mass is sufficient to provide good leverage and then examines potential tool combinations for pilot deployment.
Scope:	All IT process types, but quickly narrowed to concentrations of resource with similar support requirements.
Number of staff affected:	One or two project teams to act as test beds. A maximum of 30 people.
Potential impact:	Year 1: Minimal
Comments:	Prior to implementing an effective demand-management strategy only a small number of process areas look attractive. Localized gains are potentially significant, however, and if a suitable target process can be identified, accelerated deployment should be considered.

Initiative	***Metrics Repository***
Description:	Delay and deploy a more detailed process measurement database that will support future process-improvement efforts. This project supports both the process measurement and defect source analysis projects.
Scope:	All IT processes
Number of staff affected:	All IS staff
Potential impact:	Year 1: Minimal, until repository is populated and in use.
Comments:	Needed downstream to provide low-cost and efficient access to estimation and performance-assessment data.

Infrastructure Provisioning Portfolio

Process-Related Initiatives

Initiative	***Systems Integration***
Description:	Develop and deploy a systems-integration capability for the development and key delivery environments used by or supported by the IS organization.
Scope:	All infrastructure supported IT process types
Number of staff affected:	All users of the IS infrastructure
Potential impact:	Year 1: Will involve three to five staff full time to do the integration well, but these resources will have extensive leverage in influencing the effectiveness of development staff who use the resulting infrastructure.
Comments:	Although there may have been no major infrastructure integration defects to date, the increasing complexity of the development and implementation environments that the IS organization must support will increase the probability of a major technology-integration-related failure unless this capability is developed and available to support all IT processes.

People-Related Initiatives

Initiatives	***Create Infrastructure Management & Support Group***
Description:	Create and charter a technology support group for the development and support of the infrastructure used by the IS organization.
Scope:	All IS infrastructure
Number of staff affected:	4–5 directly. Everyone indirectly.
Potential impact:	Year 1: Target is 12–15% improvement in infrastructure availability.

Comments: An infrastructure management process will require dedicated staffing if it is to be effective. A balance will need to be struck between the need to develop specialist skills in the infrastructure support team and the need to remain focused on the support of IT processes. Staff rotation between support and development roles may be a way to address this issue.

Technology-Related Initiatives

Initiative ***Complete LAN Deployment***

Description: Complete the deployment of LAN connectivity to all IS staff in all process groups.

Scope: All IS staff groups

Number of staff affected: 250 to some extent, 85 directly.

Potential impact: Year 1: Target is 35 percent improvement in the productivity of the 85 staff who are not yet connected; 5 percent improvement in everyone once 100 percent connectivity is achieved.

Comments: Much of the effectiveness of the Year 1 program will be diminished if all staff do not have easy access to the key leverage areas of performance support and knowledge deployment.

Initiative: ***Develop an Initial Knowledge Archive on Lotus Notes***

Description: Continuation of current initiatives to develop and deploy an archive of useful reference information using *Lotus Notes* as the medium.

Scope: All IT processes

Number of staff affected: All IS staff

Potential impact: Year 1: 5% productivity improvement in all IS staff work.

Comments:	The project should include a usage monitoring capability to assess what staff find to be useful.
Initiative	***Develop and Deploy a Standard Testing Environment***
Description:	A significant proportion of IT processes involve regression testing between versions of application software. Development of a standardized set of testing tools, data sources, outcome recording, defect tracking, and issue-resolution technology would assist with both quality and productivity in this area.
Scope:	All development and enhancement processes
Number of staff affected:	200
Potential impact:	Year 1. Reduce testing hours by 30 percent and testing duration by half.
Comments:	This would be an initial area of technology leverage even if no worthwhile HPDE opportunities are identified.
Initiative	***Systems Integration Facility Development***
Description:	The system integration process should be supported by dedicated technology facilities that form a safe, isolated test bed for hardware and software integration experimentation and testing.
Scope:	IS infrastructure support processes
Number of staff affected:	15–20
Potential impact:	Year 1: 80 percent reduction in defects caused by component version changes.
Comments:	To evaluate additional infrastructure components as well as to support integration activity.

Initiatives in Subsequent Years

As the results begin to come in for the first year's program, we can develop a more detailed idea of what should be attempted in subsequent years. In general, we will want to strike a balance between continuing the improvements we achieve in Year 1 and the introduction of new programs in response to new opportunities or an increased capacity to successfully handle additional change. Table 9.4 sets out an outline of a three-year program that is built-up in this way.

Table 9.4 *Three-Year Performance-Improvement Program: Proposal Summary*

	Year 1	Year 2	Year 3
Key Themes	"Excellence in project management—get the process and infrastructure basics right."	"Optimize the development-and-delivery process and invest in selective technology leverage."	"Prepare to innovate while continuously improving."
Demand Management-related portfolio			
Process-related initiatives	New user request assessment and option appraisal process	New option appraisal process. Technology strategy review	Technology strategy review
People-related initiatives	Skills profiles and future skills demand model	Skills profile assessment and competency adjustment	Skills profile assessment and competency adjustment
Technology-related initiatives	No new platform technologies	Net fewer platform technologies	Net fewer platform technologies

(*Table continues on next page*)

Table 9.4 *(Continued)*

	Year 1	Year 2	Year 3
Process Management-related portfolio			
Process-related initiatives	Standardize Project Structuring & Planning Measurement	Process Accelerators program Dynamic management process trials	Dynamic management process deployment
People-related initiatives	PM Training and coaching Performance Incentives Program pilots	PM Training and coaching Performance Incentives Program PM improvement council	Self-managed teams pilots
Technology-related initiatives	PPA provisioning	PMA provisioning	Work-flow management
Process Execution-related portfolio			
Process-related initiatives	Standardize process Defect Source Analysis High-impact areas focus	Active process specialization	Process dynamics

Table 9.4 *(Continued)*

	Year 1	Year 2	Year 3
	Utilization monitoring review Change-management Issue management		
People-related initiatives	Process Awareness Remedial Coaching	Skills enhancement	Work-flow management
Technology-related initiatives	Performance Support HPDE Research Metrics-Repository	Performance Support HPDE deployment	Work-flow management infrastructure support
Infrastructure Provisioning-related portfolio			
Process-related initiatives	Systems Integration	Systems Integration	Implement a Reuse Outreach Process
People-related initiatives	Create infrastructure management & support group	Measure Infrastructure support effectiveness	Create infrastructure optimization group

(Table continues on next page)

Table 9.4 *(Continued)*

	Year 1	Year 2	Year 3
Technology-related initiatives	Complete LAN deployment Develop initial Knowledge Archive on *Lotus Notes* Standard Testing environment Systems Integration Facility development	HPDE development and support knowledge base development	Active infrastructure pilots

Part IV

Conclusions: How Fast Can We Really Get?

10

Really *Getting Outside the Box*

One of the incentives to write this book came in the form of a request from a client executive (not an IT executive) to take a fundamental new look at the way in which information systems are defined, built, and deployed. It was a remarkably open brief:

> *Assume that you knew nothing about how information systems have been built in the past or are being built today. Design for me a process that is only driven by the business need to have technology support immediately available for key business processes of all types. Recognize our need to change the processes quickly and to have the information technology change just as fast. Use any technology, resource and organizational assumptions you like. How fast could we really do this?*

The first thing we discovered was that it is very hard to "forget" things you already know. Subtracting 20 years of system building experience, and then giving up the mental model of what's possible as a result of this experience, proved to be extremely difficult. Those of us involved in the visioning sessions probably never managed to do so completely. But we did manage to identify and challenge a large number of the assumptions that are built-in (often invisibly) to our current processes.

Our approach was a combination of analysis within the data sets accumulated by our research and simulation modeling of new processes.[1] We recognized the weakness inherent in simulation—especially where there are very large numbers of variables involved, but we also recognized that we could not actually do all of the projects that would have been needed to examine the processes that we wanted to try out. The simulations we used seem reasonable, and were (at least initially) fairly close to other published

[1]We use as the simulation tool *ithink* from High Performance Systems Inc. of Hanover, NH. We have also used the Dynamo modeling language and tools.

work.[2,3] We validated the early models as well as we could with available experience and with research data, and went forward from there.

The more sophisticated the models became, the less "real world" data were available to validate them. In this sense, what follows is purely conceptual—a process model based on a series of "thought experiments." We have tried out many of the individual elements of the model in isolation and a few elements in various combinations. But process change implementation occurs in real time. Until we have completed an implementation of our new process in a real situation, we won't know for sure that the results promised by the simulations can really be achieved.

Overturning Preconceptions of What's Possible

When we had identified as many of the underlying assumptions about the current process as possible, we set about either reversing them (assumption reversal is a powerful visioning technique in its own right), to see what the effect would be, or redefining the process so as to eliminate or minimize their impact. The results were surprising. Software-development processes borrow a great deal from manufacturing and production-management paradigms that were relevant or even essential in the early days of computing—but apply to remarkably few areas (even areas of manufacturing) today.

[2]See *Software Project Dynamics: An Integrated Approach,* by Tarek Abdel-Hamid and Stuart E. Madnick, New York: Addison-Wesley, 1994, for an introduction to the simulation modeling approach.

[3]Although we undertook our research independently, our interest in process simulation for software projects stems from an introduction in 1993 to the excellent work of Dr. Howard Rubin and Ed Yourdon. This work is now available in the form of the Software Process Simulation Toolkit, available from Rubin Systems Inc., Pound Ridge NY.

Making the Best of the Current State

Our first attempt at improving this situation simply involved a clean-up of inefficiencies and non-value-added activities in our current processes—essentially applying all of the improvement strategies that we described in the first three parts of this book. By eliminating most of the deceleration practices and applying all of the acceleration factors that we identified in Chapters 7 and 8, and making a relatively small number of assumptions about the availability and effectiveness of infrastructure technology, we were able to design a process that should be able to build any reasonable information system in between *30 and 60 days* elapsed time.

In defining "reasonable" we restricted ourselves to project life cycles that included requirements analysis, solution design, solution development and testing, and pilot-acceptance testing. We excluded strategic information systems planning considerations and large-scale implementation phases. We also excluded projects where the primary objective was to establish and deploy extensive technology infrastructure for either development or implementation support. Finally, we excluded projects that were essentially "pure" research and development—in areas where the business problem was unknown or where emergent technology capabilities were being established.

We took for our "delivery unit" a development project that would normally (typical current state) have taken about 20,000 resource hours and lasted one elapsed year. We took a resource year to be 2,000 hours, although this is a higher number than that used by most organizations, and assumed 80 percent utilization. We assumed both a flat resource loading (10–12 resources throughout) and a stage-weighted resource loading (minimum 4, maximum 18). In most cases, we were able to show a convergence toward the flat model as cycle times compressed. In a few cases, we tried to factor-in critical resource assumptions, which almost always lengthened the cycle time (as might be expected). Finally, we modeled the cycle time impact of various types of resource change during the project.

The resulting process design scales-up well (at least in simulation) to an upper limit of about 100,000 resource hours and down to about 1,000 resource hours. Above and below these limits, a different model is required.

Above 100,000 total hours, 30 elapsed working days represents more than 400 individual resources and inter-resource communications tasks begin to dominate the work content and to create substantial instabilities in the model. Breaking the problem up into smaller pieces helps, but not much, since the constraints imposed by the overall optimization function are not affected.

Below 1,000 hours, 30 elapsed days represents at least four individual resources, but there will often be insufficient coverage of key skills or accesses to essential knowledge within the development team. Here, nonuniform resource loadings begin to dominate and critical resource availability becomes the major source of instability.

As might have been expected, we found that any change in resources during the project tended to lengthen the duration. Perhaps more surprisingly, this was the case even when a more experienced resource was being substituted for one less experienced. Integration and learning curve losses almost always outweighed the gain from additional experience.

Improvement Limits

There does, however, seem to be a practical lower limit for elapsed time of about 30 elapsed days for the best version of our improved current process. At this point, no matter what the size of the project, process synchronization requirements, inter-project resource availability, and related logistics issues introduce instabilities in the model that would almost certainly translate into schedule overruns or high defect rates in real projects.

As we continued to study the process models, looking for further improvement opportunities, it seemed clear that, to get below this level, we would need to redesign the development-and-delivery process completely.

Process Management Issues

We did, however, learn some interesting things from our simulation work that bear out results from other research in this area. Here are two.

> *Statically managed processes will always tend to exceed their elapsed time estimates if they are allowed to run to completion.*

It has become something of a mantra that good project managers "plan the work and then work the plan." This is a fine goal—so long as the path of the project can be completely determined at the outset.

In practice, there are many sources of unanticipated work, all of which tend to extend the project schedule. Beyond a certain point, adding resources slows things down (we have known this for more than 30 years, but we persist in behaving counter to this knowledge, most of the time).

While we can (and should) have change-control policies in place, and there should be related processes to manage the sources of unplanned effort, we only rarely saw circumstances in which the project's completion was not delayed, often substantially.

> *Dynamically managed processes always end earlier than the equivalent statically managed processes.*

In contrast, projects that were planned on the assumption that things would have to change in response to changing circumstances tended to end earlier than the same project managed statically. Note that the project still did not necessarily end on time, or early—just not as late as the simulation predicted for the static management scenarios.

This is comparable to the situation faced by the operators of commercial airline schedules. To be allowed to take off, pilots must file a flight plan. This defines the expected route that they will fly, but recognizes that the only fixed aspects of the flight are the start and (planned) end points. The a priori routing assumptions actually define a "safe envelope of operation" within which the actual flight is expected to occur. Going outside of this envelope without the permission of air traffic control is a violation of safety rules.

After takeoff, the pilot adjusts his route from time to time to take account of external factors such as weather, other airplane traffic, and the actions of similar variables with values that could not be predicted when the flight was planned. In doing so, he is "deviating" to some degree from his original plan, but maintaining his overall optimization objectives for the flight—safe and timely arrival at the planned destination at the best economic cost.

Clearly, factors may intervene that require a complete reevaluation of the flight plan and diversion from the original destination, but these will be low-probability events that can be handled as special cases, involving external help to resolve.

The situation is similar with dynamically managed projects (see Figure 10.1). At the start of the project, we define an expected project path and an "envelope of acceptable execution" as a part of the project plan. At the outset, there will be many possible paths that the project can take within this acceptable envelope, only one of which is the "best" prediction according to the optimization factors that we choose to apply.

As the project proceeds, the project manager works to "steer" the project as close to predicted flight path as possible, adjusting the schedule and work plan as necessary. As progress is made, an actual project "track" is established, reducing the number of the remaining paths to an acceptable conclusion. Each unit of progress that is made also redefines the envelope of acceptable paths for the remainder of the project.

As the project is brought to a conclusion, the envelope of possibilities converges to the actual project track, and we can assess how well the project did in comparison to the plan.

Our research in this area is not complete, and we are further invetigating strategies for diagnosing impending problems during

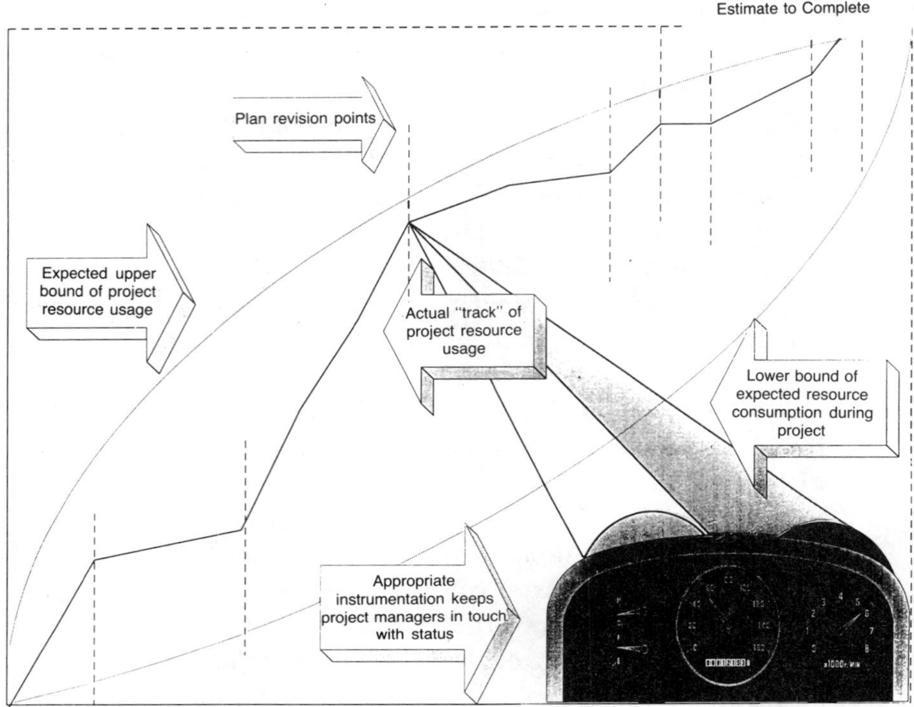

Figure 10.1 *The "envelope" of a project, and an example of a project track.*

the project (analogous to "weather radar" in our airline example). We are also investigating the effects that result from different granularities of control. Modern commercial aircraft, such as the Boeing 737-400 or Airbus Industries A320 are actually microcontrolled—the flight computers make thousands of adjustments per second to the control surfaces to keep them stable. The most modern aircraft (mostly military) cannot be flown at all unless the computers work this way, because they are aerodynamically unstable. Microcontrolled aircraft can have significantly better performance and economy than conventional designs and are believed to be just as safe.

We are following this general model with our continuing project management research.[4,5] Is there such a thing as a "microcontrolled" project, and what might it look like? If we can define a microcontrol process, is it a good idea to run projects this way, or do the response lags in the "components" (the project team and its customers) limit the control granularity that it makes sense to apply? If microcontrol is actually a good idea, what sensors and control loops do we need to make it work? These and many similar topics are directing our future research efforts.

[4] Managerial Microworlds, by P. Senge and C. Lannon. *Technology Review*, July 1990.

[5] Managing by Wire, by R. Haeckel and R. Nolan. *Harvard Business Review*, September/October 1993.

11

60 Minute Software Scenario

Any sufficiently advanced technology is indistinguishable from magic.

—ARTHUR C. CLARKE

Limits to Cycle Time Compression

Once our simulations had reduced the 30-day lower bound for a project, we went back to the limiting factors in our model and created ways either to reduce their effort or to remove them altogether. Achieving the extreme cycle time compresion in the IS development-and-delivery process that we require depends on a variety of factors that do not really exist today in an "industrial strength" combination. Most of the factors we identified do, however, exist in some form and nearly all of them are more available than most IT organizations think they are.

Here is the scenario we finally developed.

There are no longer "applications" as we think of them today—only frameworks within which to use common services.

This is the first and most significant change from "conventional" IS development thinking and is the source of our largest relative gain. If we revisit the structural analysis of application software that was described in Part I, we discover an opportunity to eliminate 95 percent to 98 percent of application-building effort at a single stroke. By providing an environment in which bundles of common 'services" do most of the work now done by application code, we eliminate from an individual project all of the effort required to develop the services themselves. We must still incur the much smaller resource penalty represented by the effort required to define and create a new framework within which the available services do useful work in support of a business process.

When we applied this reduction factor to the 30-day (240 elapsed hours) project scenario (which, of course, already contains the initial steps required for the common services approach) we felt that we could get the "development" time for this framework down to perhaps 5 percent of the 240-hour baseline, giving us a new lower bound of twelve hours.

Requirements definition, design, construction, and testing are the same process.

This is the second major source of cycle time gain. In our scenario, business users and technology providers work together to create a working example of the required solution as a part of the requirements definition and confirmation process. In essence, there are no requirements specifications other than the final deliverable of a working system. The key difference here is that this process is not simply made up of the current state-equivalent activities carried on in parallel. Instead we have a completely new process, driven from a rich set of functional examples and associated data sets, that treats all of the currently required work as integrated aspects of the same activity.

Not only do we make intensive use specification by example, but we also immediately get to see the impact of a selected example on our production data sets. By providing solution animation capabilities, using a clone of our real data, we can run "scenarios" of what the business would have been like in recent history if the new capability had been in place, as well as projecting forward the impact we might expect from the introduction of the improvements we propose to make. We may also be able to show instant parallel execution—the real-time current state alongside the "what if" version that would result from a particular solution selection.

For example, we could watch an order being taken or a customer service contact under way on our current state process at the same time as an animation of the proposed new process. Effectiveness and efficiency instrumentation, built into the infrastructure services, would give us instant measures of performance.

The gating factor we must deal with now is the speed with which we can create a stable, complete, and consistent description of a requirement for our future-state capability and get the requirement agreed by our customers. In assessing the lower limits for this, we constantly had to remind ourselves that many of the aspects of an "application" that we must now specify explicitly are no longer required. They are taken care of by the common services environment. In particular, all aspects of meta data (the data that describe the objects we are dealing with) management will be transparent to the requirements-elicitation process and we will be able to deal with abstractions of systems objects at the business level.

For example, it will not be necessary to define what we mean by "customer" or "order"—these will be predefined objects with standard behaviors that we can invoke through a standard set of business actions, see the results in real time, and request specializations to either the objects or their associated methods immediately if they are required. Methods will also be objects that can be applied wherever a specific type of behavior is required.

The complete integration of these development activities and the provision of immediate feedback to customers creates an interactive process that should provide additional efficiencies. Our estimates (we readily acknowlege that we're getting fairly conceptual here—we don't yet have a simulation model for this version of the future state) were based on looking at improvements in selection/decision-making processes resulting from interactive technology-assisted mediation in decision-making. In particular, we looked at the effect of an ability to cycle rapidly through a range of similar scenarios and converge on a preferred solution. If the gains reported in research in other fields can be applied to our future-state process, we should get at least a 50 percent reduction in cycle time and thus be able to achieve a six-hour baseline.

The next step in our compression strategy comes from optimizing the working of the decision process itself. Research on high-speed decision-making processes, much of it originally carried out for branches of the armed forces, has shown that there is an optimum order for the presentation of information relevant to a critical decision. There is also a limit to the maximum amount of information that can contribute to effective decision-making, even when additional information would, in theory, result in a better decision.

These limits vary both with the situation and the individual, and are primarily related to the limits of human ability to rapidly assimilate and integrate information into a rational decision framework. Exceeding these limits, even if value-added information is presented, reduces decision-making capability.

If we know what the relevant limits are for any given situation and for the individual participants in that situation, we can tune the information-presentation sequence and volume to get the optimum group decision in the minimum possible elapsed time. A critical factor in this process is the participant's confidence that the right information has been made available and that there are no significant omissions or misstated contexts.

Once again, it is difficult to estimate the potential improvements available from this strategy, but a further halving of the process time would mirror results achieved in high-intensity decision environments elsewhere. If we can do this, we would get down to something close to a three-hour baseline cycle time.

To get below the three-hour level, we have to make a series of reasonable, but untested, assumptions. First, we must assume that we can get further improvement through better knowledge-visualization processes and tools. There are two factors that can be worked with here. First, we can use richer presentation and interaction modalities than those we currently employ, which are relatively slow, because they need to fill in a great deal of the background context, that we should be able to eliminate.

Second, we can probably present key aspects of the system in faster than real time, without a loss of comprehensibility. This is analogous to "fast forward" on a video through the parts with which you are already familiar. A doubling of the speed of the VCR retains most of the content in a usable form. Higher speeds may be possible, but we have not assumed anything beyond $2\times$. This speed increase in some areas, plus improved visualization and presentation facilities, is the final piece of our strategy, giving us the 60-minute elapsed-time scenario which we set out to achieve.

There are four more "collateral" considerations that we will also need to make this scenario work.

There are no major closure or consistency issues that cannot be tested and resolved automatically.

We will still be restricted, to some degree, by the limitations imposed by an imprecise specification language. We therefore need a way to test the consistency and completeness of the requirements/solution combinations that result from our accelerated process. In many instances, this will not be a major issue, because the problem will be sufficiently straightforward that an exhaustive enumeration of possibilities can be undertaken within our timeline. As the levels of common services integration and interdependency grow, however, we will lose our ability to be sure that the impact of a change in the use or behavior of a common service does not create an incompatibility elsewhere.

One of the by-products of such a dramatic reduction in cycle time will be an effective increase in our capacity to build and deploy changed information systems. The impact of the many changes that we can make will have to be managed and reconciled simultaneously throughout our information infrastructure. Access to the underlying meta data definitions brings with it the need constantly to monitor definition changes, to ensure that assumptions incorporated into current applications are not being invalidated. While the version control and configuration-management technologies we have today can be used to maintain most aspects of syntactic integrity, they do not enforce semantic consistency, and Gödel's theorem suggests that no feasible technology can completely solve this problem.[1,2] In practice, it should be sufficient if we can detect that we have

[1]Think of this distinction as being similar to the analysis of a sentence in English. Syntactic consistency tells us that we have a subject, an object, a verb, and so on, but it does not prove that the sentence "means" anything. There are many examples of "nonsense" sentences that are syntactically correct.

[2]Gödel's theorem is a mathematical proposition on the impossibility of proving closure on a finite set of axioms. In essence, the theorem states that it is not possible to answer all of the questions that can legitimately be asked, based on any finite set of assumptions. The validity of the proof of this theorem has been questioned by pure mathematicians since it was first published.

caused an inconsistency and prevent mutual incompatibilities from occurring.

Teams form instantly and operate at peak effectiveness immediately.

Consider the example of an airline flight and cabin crew about to take out a commercial flight. They may never have worked together before this flight, or even know each other, yet they can come together as a functioning team within a few minutes, work together for several hours, and then disband and go on to form other teams on other flights with other "strangers." This capability does not come about by accident. Crews are trained in known competencies, recognizable infrastructure is provided, and operational processes are standardized so that the desired team behavior is possible.

We want to create the same teaming capability among our IS staff and their customers, so that they can begin effective work immediately. Notice that, in our airline crew example, the crew can be most effective only when they have experienced passengers to work with, who have also learned the essential parts of the shared process. When faced with passengers who are unfamiliar with flying in general, with the boarding process in particular, and with the most effective way to "operate as a passenger," the crew can still function well as a team, but cannot be at their most productive form. Similarly, we will need to educate our customers so that they can participate in the most productive way.

Systems integration is instantaneous.

As new business-support capability is defined and developed, it must become seamlessly integrated into the existing "production" processes and infrastructure. Development therefore must include the specification of operational policies and procedures, using a library of standard templates from which appopriate selections can be made. Software-based capabilities will have properties that define their operational needs, and defaults will be available which can be set based on the common services used, and then specialized as needed.

We will also need to manage the potential "propagation delay" that occurs when some of the common components of a complex distributed system are updated. As the system becomes larger and more complex, traditional updating methods fail, because they cannot update all of the affected components simultaneously. We must either develop rapid synchronized updating processes, or create an infrastructure that can tolerate ambiguous states, in which some instances of a component have been updated, but others have not.[3]

If we choose the former approach, then, no matter how rapid our process may be, we will eventually introduce an unacceptable performance hiatus, as the system progressively "freezes" until the final affected component enters a state from which all components can be changed. For very large and complex systems, this hiatus could be significant. We must also cope with systems in which some components are not always connected to the overall infrastructure, and so cannot always participate in a synchronized update.

If we choose the second approach, we must design all of our software so that it both reports what version it is when asked and can interrogate other components to see if they are older or newer. All components could then be made able to participate in a self-updating scheme whenever they encountered a request from a newer component or a response from an older one. We would still need to be sure that such an approach did not cause unacceptable performance degradation as system bandwidth became consumed by updating activity at the expense of supporting real work.

The target technology environment is self-adjusting.

Our final requirement concerns the ability to incorporate new implementation technology or additional capacity for the existing

[3]"Update-in-place" capabilities are already being developed and introduced for operating system components and system software.

technology infrastructure. Today there is an implementation lag caused by the need to physically adjust parts of the target technology environment to accommodate new software-based capabilities. We can eliminate or substantially reduce this lag if we make the target environment "intelligent" enough to adjust critical aspects according to measured activity. Just as, today, we can design redundancy, alternative routing, and recovery into our data networks, so should we be able to extend these types of capability to data management, processing capacity, and specialized peripherals.

If we have these additional considerations in place, we should be able to move from "requirement" to "ready to implement" within our 60-minute target time.

Moving the Bottleneck

Let's assume that we can build, or make significant changes to, business support software extremely quickly—in 60 minutes or less. What good does that do if it still takes weeks or months to implement the new capabilities?

If our future-state scenario actually works, we will be able to make dozens of changes to our installed business-support software environment every day. Imagine what this will do to the users of these capabilities. Unless we control the implementation process, the behavior of our technology could *change fundamentally and unexpectedly between one transaction and the next.* We probably don't want this to happen, at least without warning the users. On the other hand, if we really do have a better way to support some aspect of business operations, we will want to bring it into use as quickly as possible, so that the benefits that justified the change can be realized.

Improved Implementation Capability

No matter how we approach implementation, the changes we make must occur between *some* pair of transactions for every user. The first transaction gets done the old way; the second gets done the new way. We want the change to be as well synchronized as possible and to cause as little disruption as possible. In a global, constant-availability business-support environment, there may be no "good moment" for such a change to take place. We will constantly be balancing the need for synchronization (which defends the internal consistency of our processes and the infrastructure that supports them) with the need to minimize the processing delays that will occur if we make some users wait until the entire system is in a state from which we can perform a synchronized update.

Changes like this are always difficult to make today, and usually require us to create a long lead time, during which we inform those who will be affected by the change that the change is coming, what it will do, and how to get ready for it. Even then, some people fail to assimilate the warning and are "surprised" when the change actually occurs.[4] The costs associated with making this kind of implementation process effective can easily exceed the costs of development for the process and its support systems by several orders of magnitude.

[4]In 1988, a shortage of available telephone numbers forced British Telecom (BT) to introduce two new area codes for numbers in the London area, splitting the old "01" code into 071 and 081. This change was expected to have a direct impact on about 12 million people and an indirect impact on another 20 million. BT began the awareness process three months before the change and used a combination of mail (with the phone bill), billboards, press, radio, and television advertising. Their communications strategists estimated that everyone with a phone should have been exposed to the change message at least 25 times by the date of the change. Based on an analysis of connection failures and complaints during the first 24 hours after the change, only about 85 percent of phone users got the message. In April 1995, BT (and its competitors) changed the area code structure for the entire U.K., affecting about 30 million customers directly and another 20 million phone users indirectly. This time they have started the informational campaign earlier and are allowing both the old and new numbering schemes to work for the 60 days prior to the cutover date. They hope that this will get the change recognition rate up to 95 percent. Despite the increased cost of the more sophisticated implementation strategy, it will still be cheaper than a 15 percent connection failure rate on the changeover date.

Constant Implementation Concepts

In designing our future-state implementation process, we want to make an effective trade-off between the logistical difficulties associated with a major release cycle and the constant low level of disruption associated with an unending pattern of small changes that can occur at any time. It's not at all easy to see how to do this. We could use a compromise—short interval "micro-releases" on perhaps a daily basis, with an associated broadcast of the contents of the next day's release to warn users of the changes to come that will affect their work. This, at least, lets us get the users ready for a change and lets us manage the propagation-delay problem referred to earlier. Whether we can ever find a good "switchover" moment in a 24-hour constant-availability operating environment remains to be seen.

A Final Word

Although we have discovered a great deal from three-and-a-half years of accelerators research and benchmarking, we still have a long way to go in creating a real version of the sixty-minute-software scenario. We would like more information from which to investigate some of the causal issues that we have identified, but cannot readily analyze without more data from real projects. We would like to confirm that some critical aspects of our simulation models, particularly those related to stability conditions, are correct and scaleable. And we would like to develop a better model of knowledge visualization and assimilation speed.

Although our research is continuing and more data are being collected, we have detected the start of what could be two worrying trends:

1. The number of instances of a similar type of project is falling. We seem to be doing fewer comparable projects

and introducing new variables more rapidly than we had anticipated. Thus our data sets must explain even greater levels of variability in outcome with fewer cases to work from than we would like. As a result, we may *never* be able to prove the statistical validity of some of our empirical observations. This is worrisome.

2. Those who began the improvement process first are rapidly distancing themselves from everyone else in terms of their capability to sustain high performance in the development and delivery of information systems. As a result, their practices are becoming less and less like those still used by as-yet-unimproved IS organizations.

Why are these observations important? Because, how do you become really good at something when you only ever do it once or twice? And how do you learn from organizations where the processes and practices are increasingly indistinguishable from magic?

That's our research challenge for the next few years.

Appendixes

Appendix 1

Multi-Client Research Program Participants

Ernst & Young TQIM and IT Thought Leadership programs.

Ameritech*
Apple Computer*
BP Exploration
Citizens' Coke & Gas*
AT&T
Carolinas Power & Light
Corning
Eastman Kodak*
Eli Lilly*
Federal Express
First Chicago
Hewlett Packard
IBM*

*Indicates Acceleration Action Group Participant Organization.

Miliken & Company*
Owens Corning Fiberglass*
Society Bank (now the Key Services Corporation, a part of KeyCorp)*
Sun Microsystems
Texas Instruments
Xerox*

*Indicates Acceleration Action Group Participant Organization.

APPENDIX 2

Ernst & Young Carolinas IS Quality Program Participants

Burlington Industries
Coca-Cola Consolidated
First Union Bank
Northern Telecom
R.J. Reynolds
Sara Lee Hosiery
Sonoco
Springs Industries
Wachovia Financial Services
Wrangler Division of VF Corp.

APPENDIX 3

Contributing Clients and Other Sources of Research Data

Alcon Laboratories (part of Nestle SA)
Allied Signal
American Express TRS
Advanced Micro Devices
Bally Corp.
Bank One
Barclays Bank (UK)
BCTel (Canada)
Black & Decker SA (Europe)
Boeing Commercial Aircraft Group
BP Oil Europe (part of British Petroleum PLC [UK])
British Gas PLC (UK)
British Telecom PLC (UK)
Canadian International Bank of Commerce (Canada)
Capital EMI PLC (UK)
Chemical Bank
Chubb Insurance
Continental Bank (now a division of Bank of America)
Dell Computer

Dreyfus Corporation
Farmers Insurance Group (part of BAT Industries PLC)
First Data Corp.
First Direct Bank Limited (now part of the HKSB group [UK])
Gateway 2000
GE Lighting (Division of General Electric Corp.)
Georgia Pacific Corporation
GTE Telephone Operations and GTE Data Services (parts of GTE Corp.)
Grumman Data Systems
Hewlett Packard Computer Services Organization
Hoescht-Celanese Corp. (division of Hoescht gmbh)
Hughes Aerospace Corporation
Huntingdon Bankshares
Imperial Oil (Canada)
Information Systems Solutions Corp. (part of IBM Corp.)
Insurance Corporation of British Columbia (Canada)
Kobe Steel
Lockheed Corporation
LTV Steel
Massachusetts General Hospital
McDonald's Hamburgers
Microsoft
National City Bank
Nestle SA (Switzerland)
Norwich Union Life Assurance Group (UK)
Operations Development Agency (Canada)
Pacific Bell
Pacific Gas & Electric
Peidmont Natural Gas
Reynolds Metals
Rolls Royce (UK)
Sabre Travel Information Network (part of AMR Corp.)
Sapient Corporation
SeaLand Services (part of the CSX group)
Severn Trent Water Company (UK)
Schroders (UK)
Scottish Widows Life Assurance Company (UK)
Southern California Gas Corp.
Sprint
SSBA (part of MBNA Corp.)
Standard Life Assurance Company (UK)
TRW
USAA
WalMart Stores Inc.
Wheeling Pittsburgh Steel

APPENDIX 4

Process Structure and Definitions for the IT Process Landscape

Table A4.1 *IT-Enabled Business Opportunity Identification*

Purpose	To ensure that strategic business change activities fully exploit IT
Products/Services	Proposals, Assessments
Customers	Senior Business Executives
Sub-processes	Participate/Lead in Process Innovation Educate for Senior Executives in IT Possibilities Participate in Business Strategy Development Explore Emerging IT Capabilities Participate in Business Process Benchmarking

Table A4.2 *IT Infrastructure Stewardship*

Purpose	To define and design an enterprise's IT infrastructure
Products/Services	IT architectures and enterprise models
Customers	Key Stakeholders, Employees that use infrastructure
Sub-processes	Defining the IT architecture Developing and maintaining enterprise models Developing architectural standards and policies Developing knowledge bases and other repositories

Table A4.3 *IT Component Delivery and Evolution*

Purpose	To acquire, develop, and deliver new or improved hardware, software, and information components to the enterprise.
Products/Services	New or improved hardware, software, or information components
Customers	Business sponsors; component end-users
Sub-processes	Define component project Analyze business requirements Produce conceptual system design Investigate component purchase Produce technical design Purchase/build elements of component Component integration Deliver/deploy component

Table A4.4 *IT Operations*

Purpose	To support the ongoing operational requirements of the enterprise
Products/Services	Access to application systems, information warehouses, and external information sources
Customers	All users of enterprise IT
Sub-processes	Schedule IT service delivery Provide operational IT environment Control and manage IT environment Forecast volume and capacity needs Monitor status of IT environment and measure performance

Table A4.5 *IT Customer Support*

Purpose	To allow users to make more informed and effective use of IT reasoning at their service, prevent and resolve problems or questions with the IT environment
Products/Services	Training, guidance, problem resolution
Customers	All users of enterprise IT
Sub-processes	Field inquiries and manage problem resolution Provide assistance in navigating the IT environment Provide ongoing training and support

Table A4.6 *IT Strategy Development*

Purpose	To establish strategy and vision for long-term IT
Products/Services	Mission statements road maps
Customers	Key stakeholders, IS professionals
Sub-processes	Determine strategy, pacing & priorities Establish guiding IT principles/standards Manage IT costs/benefits Establish IT organizational design Establish IT HR approach

Table A4.7 *IS Management*

Purpose	To manage the business of the IS organization
Products/Services	Budgets, performance appraisals, training plans
Customers	Key stakeholders, IS professionals
Sub-processes	Create financial resources plans/budgets Fund services Measure and monitor IT performance Coordinate IT improvement activities Implement IT staffing Manage IT relationships Identify, prioritize and schedule projects

Bibliography

Most IS professionals read, on average, less than one technical book a year. The IS industry publishes well over 1,000 new titles each year. Everyone is busy, but we all need to keep current with the key concepts and trends in the industry if we are to cope with change. Here is a list of useful reference material and background reading on the various aspects of implementing an accelerated information systems development process that we have covered in this book. I have taken the liberty of marking a few of these (with an *) as "essential reading" for those of you who are going to be improvement program managers. This is my personal view—for which we make no apologies—but with which you are free to disagree after reading.

*Albrecht, A. J. (1979). Measuring Application Development Productivity. *Proceedings of the Joint SHARE/GUIDE/IBM Application Development Symposium.* Guide International Corporation.

Allen, B. (1987). Making Information Services Pay Its Way. *Harvard Business Review, 65(1).*

Andrews, D., & Leventhal, N. S. (1993). *Fusion.* Englewood Cliffs, NJ: Yourdon Press/PTR Prentice-Hall.

Arthur, L. J. (1985). *Measuring Programmer Productivity and Software Quality.* New York: John Wiley & Sons.

August, J. H. (1991). *Joint Application Design.* Englewood Cliffs, NJ: Yourdon Press/PTR Prentice-Hall.

Bailey, J. W., & Basili, V. R. (1981). A Meta-Model for Software Development and Resource Expenditures. *Proceedings of the 5th International Conference on Software Engineering.* New York: IEEE.

*Barker, J. A. (1992). *Future Edge: Discovering the New Paradigms of Success.* New York: William Morrow and Company.

*Beckhard, R., & Harris, R. (1987). *Organizational Transitions.* Reading, MA: Addison-Wesley OD Series.

*Boehm, B. (1981). *Software Engineering Economics.* Englewood Cliffs, NJ: Prentice-Hall.

*Bridgers, W. (1991). *Managing Transitions.* Reading, MA: Addison-Wesley.

*Brooks, F. P., Jr. (1982). *The Mythical Man-Month: Essays on Software Engineering.* Reading, MA: Addison-Wesley.

Buchholz, S., & Roth, T. (1987). *Creating the High-Performance Team.* New York: John Wiley & Sons.

Byham, W. C. (1989). *Zapp! The Lightning of Empowerment.*

Chen, E. T. (1978). Program Complexity and Programmer Productivity. *IEEE Transactions in Software Engineering, SE-4(3).*

Chin-Kuei Cho (1987). *An Introduction to Software Quality Control.* New York: Wiley Interscience.

*Covey, S. R. (1989). *The 7 Habits of Highly Effective People.* New York: Simon & Schuster.

Cusumano, M. A. (1991). *Japan's Software Factories.* New York: Oxford University Press.

*Davenport, T. H. (1992). *Process Innovation: Reengineering Work through Information Technology.* Boston: Harvard Business School Press.

*DeMarco, T., & Lister, T. (1987). *Peopleware: Productive Projects and Teams.* New York: Dorset House.

Drucker, P. F. (1985). *Innovation and Entrepreneurship.* New York: Harper & Row.

Egan, G. (1988). *Change Agent Skills: A—Stressing and Designing*

Excellence; B—Managing Innovation and Change. University Associates.

Gilb, T. (1977). *Software Metrics.* Winthrop Publishers.

Gilb, T. (1988). *Principles of Software Engineering Management.* Reading, MA: Addison-Wesley.

Glass, R. L. (1992). *Building Quality Software.* Englewood Cliffs, NJ: Prentice-Hall.

Goldratt, E. M., & Cox, J. (1984). *The Goal: A Process of Ongoing Improvement.* North River Press.

*Grady, R. B. (1992). *Practical Software Metrics for Project Management and Process Improvement.* Englewood Cliffs, NJ: PTR Prentice-Hall.

*Grady, R. E., & Casewell, D. (1987). *Software Metrics: Establishing a Company-wide Program.* Englewood Cliffs, NJ: Prentice-Hall.

*Hammer, M., & Champy, J. (1993). *Reengineering the Corporation. A Manifesto for Business Revolution.* New York: Harper Business.

Jones, T. C. (1981). *Programming Productivity: Issues for the Eighties.* IEEE Catalog No. EHO 186-7. New York: IEEE.

Jones, T. C. (1986). *Programming Productivity.* New York: McGraw-Hill.

*Katzenbach, J. R., & Smith, D. K. (1987). *The Wisdom of Teams.* Boston: Harvard Business School Press.

Keen, P. G. W. (1988). *Competing in Time.* New York: Harper Business.

Longworth, G. (1987). *Realistic User Requirements.* Manchester, England: NCC Publications.

Martin, J. (1987). *Information Engineering.* Englewood Cliffs, NJ: Prentice-Hall.

*McGee, J., & Prusak, L. (1993). *Managing Information Strategically.* New York: John Wiley & Sons.

Merlyn, V., & Parkinson, J. (1994). *Development Effectiveness: Strategies for IS Organizational Transition.* New York: John Wiley & Sons.

Meyer, C. (1993). *Fast Cycle Time: How to Align Purpose, Strategy, and Structure for Speed.* New York: Free Press.

Morton, M. S. S. (Ed.) (1991). *The Corporation of the 1990s: Information Technology and Organizational Transformation.* New York: Oxford University Press.

Norman, D. A. (1988). *The Design of Everyday Things.* New York: Basic Books.

Olsen, D. (1993). *Exploiting Chaos.* New York: VNR Computer Library, Van Nostrand Reinhold.

Pagals, H. R. (1989). *The Dreams of Reason: The Computer and the Rise of the Sciences of Complexity.* New York: Bantam Books.

Parker, M. M., & Benson, R. J. (1988). *Information Economics.* Englewood Cliffs, NJ: Prentice-Hall.

Parkinson, J. (1991). *Making CASE Work.* Manchester, England: NCC Blackwell.

Prahalad, C. K., & Hamel, G. (1990). The Core Competence of the Corporation. *Harvard Business Review*, May/June 1990.

Putnam, L. H. (1980). *Software Cost Estimating and Life-Cycle Control: Getting the Software Numbers.* IEEE Catalog No. EHO 165-1. New York: IEEE.

Richard, F. (1986). *Innovation: The Attacker's Advantage.* London: Macmillan.

Robinson, J. R. (1991). *The Software Factory: Managing Software Development and Maintenance.* Wellesley, MA: QED Information Sciences, Inc.

Schaefer, R. H. (1988). *The Breakthrough Strategy.* New York: Harper Business.

Schein, E. H. (1988). *Planning and Managing Change. Management in the 1990s.* Boston: Sloan School of Management, Massachusetts Institute of Technology.

Schur, S. G. (1994). *The Database Factory.* New York: John Wiley & Sons.

Schwartz, P. (1991). *The Art of the Long View.* New York: Doubleday.

*Senge, P. M. (1990). *The Fifth Discipline: The Art and Practice of the Learning Organization*. New York: Doubleday/Currency.

Stalk, G., Jr., & Hout, T. M. (1990). *Competing against Time*. New York: Free Press.

*Tuttle, T., & Sink, D. (1984). Taking the Threat Out of Productivity Measurement. *National Productivity Review*.

Weinberg, G. M. (1993). *Quality Software Management: Volume 1—Systems Thinking*. New York: Dorset House.

Weinberg, G. M. (1993). *Quality Software Management: Volume 2—First Order Measurement*. New York: Dorset House.

Womack, J. P., Jones, D. T., & Roos, D. (1991). *The Machine That Changed the World: The Story of Lean Production*. New York: Harper Perennial.

Zachman, J. (1986). *A Framework for Information Systems Architecture, G320-2785*. IBM Corporation.

Index